Technical

Style

J. M. Haile

MACATEA PRODUCTIONS • CENTRAL, SOUTH CAROLINA

Published by Macatea Productions, Central, South Carolina, USA.

http://www.macatea.com/

contact@macatea.com

Library of Congress Control Number: 2001097283

Publisher's Cataloging-in-Publication Data:

Haile, J. M.
    Technical style / J.M. Haile. -- 1st ed.
    p. cm.
    Includes bibliographical references and index.
    ISBN 0-9715418-0-9

    1. Technical writing--Handbooks, manuals, etc.
 I. Title.

T11.H35 2001   808'.0666
                                 QBI01-201356

Printed on acid-free paper by
DeHart's Printing Services Corporation, Santa Clara, California, USA

6 5 4 3 2 1

Preface

If writing had not been invented, then science and technology could certainly not have advanced to their present levels of importance in modern life. Writing serves as a kind of collective memory: it records what has been learned and communicates that learning to others, including future generations. Writing clarifies thought, for it enables us to convert ideas and chains of logic from the world of fuzzy mental abstraction to the world of visible and tangible reality. Further, writing allows us to create hypothetical worlds. Through written documents we propose new machines, new processes, new societies, and then we use additional written documents to test whether those propositions are in fact possible or desirable.

But for technical documents to serve these important—nay, crucial—roles, the writing must be accurate and accessible to readers. Accuracy and accessibility—those are our watchwords, for if the writing is inaccurate, then it is either inconsequential or dangerous, and if it is inaccessible, then it is irrelevant. Accuracy and accessibility signal a good technical style.

How does technical style differ from other styles of writing? In terms of use of language, very little. The principal guidelines for achieving good English usage apply to technical writing, but technical writing also uses devices besides language, devices such as equations, tables, and figures. The accomplished writer must control not only the language, but also these other devices. Moreover, the writer must use these devices, not as isolated objects, but in concert; text, equations, tables, and figures must all interconnect to provide distinct, but overlapping, aspects of a technical story. Unfortunately, these devices are often neglected, or at least relegated to secondary roles, by many books and instructors of technical writing.

But we should not criticize earlier authors and teachers too severely, for the act of writing has changed. In earlier years the preparation of a technical document was a collaborative affair: the scientist or engineer concentrated on content, an experienced typist worried about format and grammar, and a draftsman prepared figures. Now this collaboration has been supplanted by the personal computer; instead of having three people involved, we have just one. And so while the computer has made writing in some sense more efficient, the demands on the one remaining individual are greater. This exemplifies the Law of Unintended Consequences: although one intended use of computers was to make writing easier, in fact, today's technical writers must be more knowledgeable and versatile than before, for they must confront *all* aspects of document preparation—form as well as content.

This problem is not alleviated by the availability of software for graphic design and word processing. To reach a general audience, software must present numerous options, but many of these options are inappropriate or actually detrimental to good technical writing. So, in choosing from among those options, writers must exercise good judgment.

Judgment determines style, and the themes of this book are that an effective style is achieved when judgment is guided by the following considerations: (1) The goal of technical style is to help the reader get the message. Even grammatically correct text is wrong if it hinders communication. (2) Likewise, equations, tables, and figures should be *designed* to facilitate communication. The structural forms used for these devices should be as transparent as possible, for the reader should be drawn to the message, not to the way the message is conveyed. (3) An important aspect of any good design is economy—the materials used should be appropriate to the job at hand, redundancies should be eliminated, and every part should contribute to the whole.

These comments also apply to writing. (4) Good technical writing proceeds by trial and error, so all aspects of the work—text, equations, tables, and figures—must be scrupulously edited to remove flaws.

Much of the advice in this book is offered within the context of examples, examples good and bad. When examples of poor usage are presented, they are critiqued and revised. In Chapters 1-4 the examples of strong and weak usage are displayed on lines separate from the text, and they are numbered in the margin. The numbers are prefixed with either an E or an R to distinguish an example from its subsequent revision; thus,

> Last but not least, all of these aspects of modeling   (E0.1)
> are addressed and successfully resolved in the
> development of the two methods and evaluated
> on several representative problems.

can be clarified by writing

> Finally, these issues are resolved by the methods   (R0.1)
> developed here; to demonstrate this claim, the
> two new methods are tested on several
> representative problems.

Most of the sample sentences, paragraphs, equations, tables, and figures were taken from student theses—documents labored over by graduate students and then checked and approved by faculty committees. Apparently, students are not the only ones who should devote more attention to communication skills.

In presenting the examples of poor usage, I confess to some editing. The editing took two forms: (a) Many of the original excerpts contained multiple problems, and to keep a discussion focused on the problem at hand, I corrected or eliminated distracting issues. (b) Since the intention in presenting the examples is to instruct, not embarrass, I have tried to protect the identities of the guilty by occasionally using common nouns in place of obscure and specialized ones. The basic weak structures were unaltered, only nouns were replaced; this innocent diversion sometimes produced rather delightful consequences.

In the course of reading the many theses that provided the background for this book, I was struck that, while some writers have severely underdeveloped writing skills, in fact many have few problems. Often an individual had as few as half-a-dozen idiosyncrasies, but the individual consistently repeated those same six mistakes. If this observation is generally true, then it is a cause for optimism, for it suggests that, with modest efforts, we could substantially improve the documents produced by many technical writers. The possibilities for such improvements motivate this work; may the effort help you at least a little.

Acknowledgments

It is a pleasure to thank those who took time to read and criticize various drafts of this work. The student perspective was given by Cheryl P. Hollowell and Paul Frymier. Views representing instructors in technical communication were offered by Kathryn A. Neeley, Melvin Cherno, and Arthur Young. Technical details were checked by Sohail Murad.

I am grateful to the following authors for their kind permission to reproduce excerpts from their publications: P. W. Atkins, H. Petroski, and E. O. Wilson. Additional permissions were granted by Harry N. Abrams, Inc., Cambridge University Press, and the Chemical Engineering Division of the American Society of Engineering Education.

Contents

Engineers

... make mistakes in their assumptions,
in their calculations, in their conclusions.
That they make mistakes is forgivable;
that they catch them is imperative.
Thus it is the essence of modern engineering
not only to be able to check one's own work,
but also to have one's work checked
and to be able to check the work of others.
In order for this to be done,
the work must follow certain conventions,
conform to certain standards,
and be an understandable piece
of technical communication.

Henry Petroski, *To Engineer is Human*, Vintage Press, 1992. Reprinted with permission from Henry Petroski.

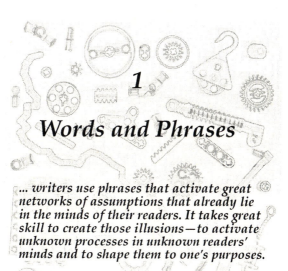

1

Words and Phrases

... writers use phrases that activate great networks of assumptions that already lie in the minds of their readers. It takes great skill to create those illusions—to activate unknown processes in unknown readers' minds and to shape them to one's purposes.

Minsky [1]

Our goal is this: to write clearly, precisely, economically—not to entreat, nor impress, nor even entertain—but simply to communicate. To reach our goal we must be sensitive to words, so that we choose the appropriate word and place it correctly in its sentence; we must be imaginative, so that we anticipate how a phrase might lead a reader astray; we must be self-critical, so that we can edit our own work; and we must read good authors, so that we develop an appreciation for proper usage. Our goal is difficult to achieve, but so are all worthwhile pursuits. We begin by considering usage that leads to strong sentences—we aim to combine words and phrases into sentences that are clear, precise, economical.

1.1 SENTENCE ELEMENTS

To write sentences that are strong and effective, we must do more than merely combine words and phrases in grammatically correct ways. We must start with carefully chosen words and then arrange those words to achieve clarity and precision. In this section we discuss how sentences are affected by the selection and arrangement of their principal elements: verbs (§ 1.1.1), nouns (§ 1.1.2), and modifiers (§ 1.1.3).

1.1.1 VERBS

Strong sentences are built around strong verbs, verbs that suggest motion or growth or change. All verbs connect the subject to the rest of the sentence, but strong verbs make that connection concrete and dynamic. In contrast, weak verbs lack a sense of motion or change. The weakest verbs merely denote states of being or existence and therefore include all the forms of *to be*, when standing alone. Consider this example:

> The viscosity of pancake syrup is dependent upon (E1.1)
> its temperature.

Here we have a simple statement of fact, but the sentence not only conveys little information, it is also dull. In (E1.1) nothing happens that might capture the reader's interest—the viscosity, the pancake, the syrup are all just there, and they are there abstractly. Here is a revision,

> The viscosity of pancake syrup decreases when (R1.1)
> its temperature increases.

Now we have a little action: something goes up, something else goes down. By using active verbs, we tacitly invite readers to relate the action to their own experiences—Oh yes, I know about trying to pour cold syrup from a bottle, if you want it to flow easily, warm it up! At least our revision gives readers an opportunity to call on their experiences, while the original gives readers no chance at all.

Good writing holds interest by creating images in the minds of its readers, and images are more likely to spring from sentences that are dynamic rather than inert. Dynamic images are routinely used to stimulate interest in television programming; those same stimulants can also be used to make the written word more effective.

Strong verbs not only help hold interest, but they can also help us be more precise. Note that (E1.1) doesn't tell us *how* the viscosity changes with temperature; the sentence leaves unspecified whether the syrup flows more easily or less easily when the temperature is increased. In contrast, by using a stronger verb, we have made the revision (R1.1) more informative than the original, and we have done so *with the same number of words.*

Unfortunately, in technical writing we must rely, to some extent, on weak verbs because often we are indeed simply reporting the existence of things, events, or relations. Thus our writing contains many sentences that use some form of *to be*, standing alone, and such usage cannot be gracefully avoided. But this should not deter us from using strong verbs wherever we can. We should compensate for unavoidable statements of existence by eliminating those weak verbs that have crept into our writing unnecessarily.

Caution: You may create an unintended image if you couple an active verb to an inanimate subject that cannot perform the stated action. For example,

> Ventilation hoods insert a measure of safety (E1.2)
> into chemistry labs.

No, not at all: ventilation hoods are incapable of inserting an abstraction (safety) into anything. Such a sentence will likely create discomfort in the minds of most readers, and discomfort promotes distraction, which in turn leads to lost readers. Sensitive readers will detect the falseness of the image and the writer's credibility will suffer. Here's a revision,

> In chemistry labs, ventilation hoods protect (R1.2)
> researchers from hazardous fumes.

Again, by finding an appropriate verb, we have made the revision (R1.2) more precise than the original (E1.2) without increasing the number of words.

1.1.2 Nouns

If the strength of the verb supports the weight of the sentence, then the weight itself resides mainly in the nouns. Don't overburden your sentences with weighty nouns; your aim is to balance the nouns against the verbs. Paradoxically, weak verbs usually invoke weighty nouns; otherwise, the sentence would carry little meaning. Consider,

> The resolution in the range of magnification (E1.3)
> of the microscope was not high enough
> for the determination of pore structures.

Here the single verb is overwhelmed by a massive structure that hides a simple thought:

> The microscope failed to resolve pore structures. (R1.3)

Not only is (E1.3) wordy, but it also contains strong verbs—resolve, magnify, determine—disguised as nouns. The resulting sentence is weak, unbalanced, overblown. Perhaps the writer was motivated by a mistaken idea of formality, but more likely (E1.3) is simply the product of bad habits.

Here is a more subtle example,

> The process is also used to draw comparisons (E1.4)
> between French models and other European
> modeling techniques.

This sentence has multiple problems, including a verb (compare) disguised as a noun. To strengthen (E1.4), remove the weak verb (is used) and unmask the hidden strong verb; thus,

The process also allows French models to be (R1.4)
compared with other European models.

Williams [2] refers to nouns created from verbs as *nominalizations*; Webster's Dictionary [3] refers to them as *verbal nouns*. Examples include convergence, conversion, comparison, development, and relationship. Weighty verbal nouns are often formed by adding the suffix *-tion*; thus we have application, association, accumulation, aggregation, definition, determination, derivation, equation, examination, experimentation, inclusion, optimization, prediction, production, relation, and resolution. Here is another example,

These steps may contribute to the limitation (E1.5)
in chemical reaction speed.

and its revision,

These steps may limit the speed of the (R1.5)
chemical reaction.

But such poor usage is not restricted to weighty nouns. Verbs can also be converted into adjectives, either directly (depend → dependent, observe → observable) or indirectly via verbal nouns (calculate → calculation → calculational). Here is a sentence weakened by a verbal adjective,

Almost no change was observable in this test. (E1.6)

We improve the sentence by converting the adjective to a verb,

In this test little change was observed. (R1.6)

As a last example consider this,

The novelty of this calculational technique is that (E1.7)
only a small amount of experimentation is needed.

Notice how the weak verb, verbal adjective, and verbal noun combine to obscure the writer's failure in distinguishing means from ends. Presumably it's not the experiments that are wanted, but the results from the experiments:

This calculation requires little experimental data.   (R1.7)

Verbal nouns and verbal adjectives are often coupled to weak verbs, so we have the following strategy for editing [2]:

(i)   identify those sentences having weak verbs,
(ii) find the verbal noun or verbal adjective,
(iii) convert verbal nouns back to verbs; convert verbal adjectives to nouns or verbs, or eliminate them altogether, then
(iv) recast the sentence.

This procedure was followed in revising each example offered above. As a result, all our revisions are stronger, more precise, and easier to read than their original counterparts. Moreover, each revision uses fewer words than its original: we have done more with less—the true test of economy.

1.1.3 MODIFIERS

In technical writing, adjectives, adverbs, and prepositional phrases serve primarily as qualifiers: they allow us to be precise rather than vague. If your writing is to be factual and clear, then you must choose your modifiers so that they are used to good advantage. If your writing is to be crisp and to the point, then you must omit modifiers that are fuzzy or uninformative. When in doubt, leave it out.

1.1.3.1 ADVERBS

In formal technical writing we should restrict the use of such adverbs as *enormously, extremely, greatly, quite,* and *very.* First, we have the obligation to be specific whenever possible: not "it was very cold", but "the temperature was 4°C". Second, we should strive for objectivity: you may think it very cold, but an Eskimo may think it balmy. Vagueness and subjectivity undermine credibility.

1.1.3.2 ADJECTIVES

Few structures impede comprehension more thoroughly than an excessive build-up of adjectives; for example,

> In this thesis a least squares based model   (E1.8)
> predictive algorithm is developed.

What could this mean? Is it the model that is predictive, or is it a predictive algorithm? Is the sentence about a model algorithm or about an algorithmic model? Is it the model or the algorithm that is based on least squares? Only the cognoscenti could possibly understand such a sentence, and presumably they have no need to read it. Here's another, even worse,

> A multi-step time-lag recurrent radial basis   (E1.9)
> function optimal network was used.

Of the eleven words in this sentence, eight (72%) are modifiers. Such a sentence defies comprehension; moreover, it has a machine-gun cadence that grates on the ear—try reading it aloud. Such constructions will frustrate and antagonize readers, forcing them to seek more congenial authors.

Adjectives are always singular, which is a point to keep in mind when using nouns as adjectives. Thus we write "ten-yard line", "man-made fibers", and "two-node network"—not "two-nodes network". This rule seems simple, but applying it can involve complexities. For example, when a noun N falls between a number and another noun (e.g., five-string banjo), then N acts as an adjective and it is *always* singular. But when a noun falls between a number and an adjective, then the noun acts as an adverb and it may be either singular or plural, depending on whether the number is greater than or equal to one. Thus the following sentence is grammatically correct:

> A three-foot board does not necessarily contain   (E1.10)
> three board feet; it is merely three feet long.

Pay special attention when a noun forms its plural in an irregular way. For example, we write

> Willard Gibbs laid the theoretical foundations   (E1.11)
> for solving all phase equilibrium problems.

Writing "equilibria problems" would be wrong. For a list of common technical nouns that form their plurals without adding s, see Table 1.1.

This brings us to the troublesome four-letter word *data*, which is one of the plural forms of the Latin noun *datum*. When used as a subject, *data* takes a plural verb, unless it is absolutely clear that a collection of data is being discussed as a single unit. If you have any doubt, use the plural verb.

But formally it is wrong to use *data* as an adjective. However, we all know that it is commonly used as an adjective: "data point" and "data set" pervade the technical literature. Even Webster's acknowledges "data bank" and "data processing" as in common use [3]. But you should consider whether you want your work, a formal piece of writing, to contain phrases that are commonly accepted, but formally wrong. I won't try to force this issue, I merely bring it to your attention. I restrain myself on this point because I believe I have a stronger argument.

My argument is that the phrases "data point" and "data set" are each redundant. Why write

> In Figure 179 the experimental data set is   (E1.12)
> plotted as a sequence of points, and the
> line, which represents our theory, passes
> through all the data points.

when all you need is this:

> In Figure 179 the experimental data are plotted   (R1.12)
> as points, and the line, which represents our
> theory, passes through all the points.

Leaving grammatical correctness aside, *data* should rarely, if ever, be used as an adjective because doing so is unnecessary and therefore not economical.

Table 1.1
Selected Nouns that Form Plurals Without Adding s

Singular	Plural	Singular	Plural
abscissa	abscissae	bacterium	bacteria
alga	algae	datum	data
antenna	antennae	equilibrium	equilibria
formula	formulae	extremum	extrema
hyperbola	hyperbolae	maximum	maxima
nebula	nebulae	medium	media
parabola	parabolae	minimum	minima
annulus	annuli	momentum	momenta
bacillus	bacilli	optimum	optima
fungus	fungi	phylum	phyla
locus	loci	quantum	quanta
modulus	moduli	stratum	strata
nucleus	nuclei	criterion	criteria
radius	radii	phenomenon	phenomena

1.1.3.3 ARTICLES

The is the definite article; it implies a particular one. *A* and *an* are indefinite and imply any one. Americans seem to use too many articles, frequently inserting *the* when no article is required. Many other writers tend to omit articles that are required; this seems especially true of those whose native languages have no articles. Be aware.

The choice of the indefinite article depends on the sound of the following syllable: *an* should precede vowel sounds, *a* should precede the rest. Thus, you should write

> At a university gift shop, she bought an umbrella (E1.13)
> with a unique shape.

and

> He broke an hour glass by hitting it with a (E1.14)
> hammer.

This rule applies when the sound of the following syllable is given by a letter; thus, write "an FNN", "an N-body problem", "an RBN", "an LED", but "a UHF radio".

1.1.3.4 PREPOSITIONAL PHRASES

Just as an extended sequence of adjectives can be ambivalent, so too can an uninterrupted series of prepositional phrases. For example,

> Corn meal was obtained from Bob's Mill by (E1.15)
> cryogenic grinding of yellow field corn.

You may feel that this sentence is clear, only a little awkward, but consider, Who did the grinding?

To be effective and forestall ambiguities, prepositional phrases must be placed near the words they modify. This suggests the idea of linkage: the preservation of proper relations among words, especially between nouns and their modifiers, subjects and verbs, and pronouns and their antecedents. In strong sentences, all elements are firmly and clearly linked. Ultimately the linkage is logical, but in English linkage is communicated by the order in which elements are presented. To avoid the poor linkage that can result from a sequence of prepositional phrases, adhere to the Rule of Three: *Write no more than three uninterrupted prepositional phrases in a row, rarely even three.*

In (E1.15) the three prepositional phrases obscure how the last two are linked to the rest of the sentence. Is *by* supposed to link to Bob's Mill, or to the verb *obtained*, or to the unidentified person who obtained the meal? As readers we can only guess. As writers we must avoid maneuvering readers into such traps of ambivalence, else we defeat the purpose of writing.

Linkage is often problematic when two or more prepositional phrases follow a verbal noun. Consider the following such structures, which commonly appear in technical writing:

> approximation of A by B
> comparison of A with B
> determination of the effect of A on B
> relationship between A and B
> separation of A from B

If A and B are each long clauses, or if they are each composed of several phrases, then the sentence may be ambivalent, and the reader must make a determined effort to identify how A is related to B. For example, here we have a sequence of five prepositional phrases:

> The determination of the effect of a structural   (E1.16)
> breakdown during the low frequency test on
> the response curve of the high frequency test
> is shown in Figure 7.

When A and B are each short (two or three words), then it may be sufficient to remove one prepositional phrase by converting the verbal noun to the infinitive:

approximation of A by B	→	to approximate A by B
comparison of A with B	→	to compare A with B
relationship between A and B	→	to relate A to B
separation of A from B	→	to separate A from B
determination of the effect of A on B	→	to determine the effect of A on B

But when A and B are long, as in (E1.16), then the Rule of Three usually requires more drastic measures. In such situations, convert the verbal noun to its verb and place it between A and B:

approximation of A by B	→	A is approximated by B
comparison of A with B	→	A is compared with B
relationship between A and B	→	how A is related to B
separation of A from B	→	A is separated from B
determination of the effect of A on B	→	to determine how A affects B

Thus (E1.16) could be revised to read

> Figure 7 shows how a structural breakdown during the low frequency test affects the response curve of the high frequency test.　　　(R1.16)

This revision contains only two prepositional phrases, and each immediately follows the word it modifies.

1.2 Avoid Conflicts in Number

In every sentence the verb must agree in number with its subject. To satisfy this rule we must identify the subject and determine whether it is singular or plural. When the writer incorrectly identifies the subject, the result may be a real conflict in number between the subject and its verb (§ 1.2.1). But when the reader incorrectly identifies the subject, the result may be an apparent conflict—the sentence is grammatically correct, but it seems wrong (§ 1.2.2). To avoid real conflicts, writers need merely pay attention to grammatical rules, but to avoid creating apparent conflicts, writers must anticipate how a sentence can lead readers astray.

1.2.1 REAL CONFLICTS

Many conflicts in number occur because the writer has failed to recognize (i) that some nouns form their plurals without adding s, or (ii) that some collective nouns may be singular or plural, or (iii) that a few nouns are usually singular even though they end in s.

Plural without s. We have already encountered *data* as a problematical plural noun (§ 1.1.3.2). Table 1.1 lists others that often appear in technical writing; still others are common to particular specialties, such as the biological sciences.

Singular or plural. More troublesome are collective nouns, such as *number* and *variety,* that may be singular or plural, depending on context. *Number* is singular when referring to a group as a single entity:

> In our lab the number of computers has increased. (E1.17)

But it is plural when used to refer to individual members of the group,

> A number of computers have been added to (E1.18)
> our lab.

Sometimes the article guides us to the correct choice of verb; for example, in (E1.17) *the number* takes a singular verb, because *the number* refers to *the total,* which is the entire collection. But in (E1.18) *a number* takes a plural verb, because *a number* refers to *many.*

However, the article is not always a reliable guide, and in such cases, context determines selection of the verb. For example,

> A variety of computers is available at the store.   (E1.19)

This sentence states that the store offers only one kind of computer. In contrast,

> A variety of computers are available at the store.   (E1.20).

means that the store offers many kinds of computers. Either (E1.19) or (E1.20) could be correct (or wrong), depending on context.

Beware of nouns such as *class, group,* and *set* which always refer to a collection as an entity; they never refer to individual members, and therefore they always take singular verbs. Careless writers, however, may use them to refer to individuals and apply a singular verb, creating a double error—but in writing, two wrongs compound, they never cancel.

Usually singular but end in s. Nouns of this class include those that end in -ics, for example *dynamics, kinetics, mathematics, physics,* and *statistics.* These nouns are singular when used to refer to a discipline or an organized area of study.

> Nonlinear dynamics is now being applied to   (E1.21)
> many problems beyond mathematical physics.

But they may be plural when used to refer to particular activities or situations,

> Planetary dynamics are now understood to   (E1.22)
> such an extent that even the motions of
> asteroids can be predicted reliably.

If you are unconvinced of any difference in number between (E1.21) and (E1.22), try replacing "dynamics" with "motion."

Then (E1.21) would read "Nonlinear motion is ..." but (E1.22) should read "Planetary motions are ...".

1.2.2 APPARENT CONFLICTS

Apparent conflicts in number can be more insidious than real conflicts because the problem is not usually grammatical but syntactical. For example,

> In the previous chapter the standard form for (E1.23)
> computational algorithms was introduced.

This sentence is grammatically correct ("form was introduced"), but it presents an apparent conflict ("algorithms was").

Whenever we try to digest technical material, concentration is paramount. Any spontaneous break in concentration can frustrate our attempts to assimilate and comprehend; if frustration accumulates, we will lose the thread of the presentation. Distraction may be caused by either a real or an apparent lapse in proper usage. Thus, just as actual errors can harm our message, so too can apparent errors. Both can distract readers from *what* we are trying to say, to *how* we are saying it. Any such shift in the reader's attention subverts communication.

In (E1.23) the apparent error occurs because the verb is poorly linked to its subject. The subject and verb are separated by a phrase, and the reader—anticipating that linkage is reinforced by proximity—tries to link the singular verb to the closest noun, which happens to be plural. To emphasize proper linkage, develop the habit of placing verbs physically close to their subjects. Thus, we edit (E1.23) to this,

> The previous chapter introduced the standard (R1.23)
> form for computational algorithms.

To help the reader get our message, we must anticipate and guard against both real and apparent errors. In other words, grammatical correctness is only a necessary condition for effective writing, it is not sufficient. A strong sentence is in this way like Caesar's wife: not only must it *be* correct, but it must also *appear* to be correct.

1.3 KEEP PARALLEL STRUCTURES STRICTLY PARALLEL

Parallelism is a rhetorical device in which a grammatical structure is repeated for emphasis or economy or both. An example occurs at the end of Lincoln's Gettysburg address,

> ... government of the people, by the people,   (E1.24)
> for the people ...

Parallelism achieves emphasis and economy by establishing a recognizable pattern that allows words, phrases, or whole clauses to be omitted without loss of clarity.

Omitting words is an obvious way to achieve economy, but it may be less obvious that omission can also add emphasis, thereby strengthening a sentence. In part, omission contributes to emphasis by concentrating the message in a smaller package: verbosity dilutes the message. But in addition, emphasis can sometimes be enhanced by omitting selected words so that the remaining words repeat a grammatical pattern; in such cases, emphasis is attained through repetition. An example occurs in the following collection of words, perpetrated by Hofstadter [4]:

> This sentence no verb.   (E1.25)

Here the repeated adjective-noun pattern provokes the reader to mentally supply the missing verb. By such repeated patterns we can entice the reader into a kind of literary interpolation in which a passive calling of words is transformed into an active engagement of the mind. But the interpolation will prove faulty, and readers may be led astray, unless we maintain grammatical consistency among all parallel parts.

1.3.1 EXCLUSIVE AND INCLUSIVE PAIRS

Exclusive pairs take the form "... either A or B ... ", while inclusive pairs are of the form " ... not only A but also B." In both uses, the grammatical structure of A and B must be identical; although, if A is long, B may take an abbreviated form of the structure used in A. The test for correctness is easy: the sentence must remain grammatically sound when the positions of A and B are reversed. That is, we must have these equivalences,

$$\text{either A or B} \quad\Leftrightarrow\quad \text{either B or A}$$
$$\text{not only A but also B} \quad\Leftrightarrow\quad \text{not only B but also A.}$$

Consider the following example,

> This is accomplished by either changing the (E1.26a)
> flow rate or the concentration.

Applying our test, we have

> This is accomplished by either the concentration (E1.26b)
> or changing the flow rate.

The sentence fails: A and B are not identical structures. To correct the original (E1.26a), we have at least three choices. One is to make A and B both objects of the gerund,

> This is accomplished by changing either the (R1.26a)
> flow rate or the concentration.

The second choice is to repeat *changing*, thereby making A and B both objects of the preposition,

> This is accomplished by either changing the   (R1.26b)
> flow rate or changing the concentration.

The third choice is to make A and B both prepositional phrases,

> This is accomplished either by changing the   (R1.26c)
> flow rate or by changing the concentration.

When A and B are both short, as in this example, then the first revision (R1.26a) is preferred. But when A and B are long, then either (R1.26b) or (R1.26c) is better because, after a long phrase, repeating a word reinforces the parallelism. See § 1.3.3 below.

We recognize that "or" is exclusive, but sometimes we want to use "or" with inclusive pairs. This poses a dilemma that many writers resolve by writing "A and/or B". But no one actually says such an ugly thing as "A and/or B", so why write it? Instead, write "either A or B or both".

1.3.2 PROCEDURES

Another common use of parallelism occurs when we recite the steps required to perform some action. Parallelism is achieved by using the same grammatical skeleton for all enumerated steps. This can be tested by checking whether each step makes an acceptable sentence if it alone is appended to any phrases that apply to all steps. Here is an example,

> The procedure was (1) calculate the temperature   (E1.27)
> and concentration, (2) using Newton's method
> calculates an effectiveness factor, and (3) global
> rates may then be calculated from Equation 10.

To test this for parallelism, we check whether a sentence is formed from the preparatory phrase plus each individual step. For example, the test involving the third step gives

> The procedure was global rates may then be calculated from Equation 10.

This fails. The second step of example (E1.27) also fails. To correct (E1.27) we note that the pattern to be repeated has the skeletal form (verb + direct object), so we revise (E1.27) to

> The procedure was (1) calculate the temperature (R1.27)
> and concentration, (2) calculate an effectiveness
> factor using Newton's method, and (3) calculate
> global rates from Equation 10.

Procedures convey an air of authority if each step begins, as (R1.27) does, with an imperative verb. Here is a properly constructed example, which addresses maintenance of diesel engines on small sailboats:

> (a) Lay a clean towel over the stern lifeline. (E1.28)
> (b) Go to engine compartment and decouple drive
>   shaft from propeller shaft.
> (c) Remove all mounting bolts.
> (d) Lift engine from base.
> (e) Carry engine topside to the stern lifeline.
> (f) Swing and heave.
> (g) Use towel to mop the splash.

1.3.3 SEQUENCES OF SUBORDINATE CLAUSES

Parallel clauses may pose problems merely because their lengths can obscure the parallelism. Often the problems can be solved by repeating one or more words—repetition can reinforce parallelism. Consider this wordy example,

> It is hoped that the results obtained can be used (E1.29)
> to form predictions of what effects similar
> additives will have on the mixtures and how
> these changes will affect the process.

In this sentence the parallelism is not obvious and therefore not effective; worse, it fails to adhere to a standard form and so it seems to be grammatically questionable. Part of the problem is that the main clause leads the reader to expect the form

It is hoped that A and B.

But this form does not appear in (E1.29). Some searching reveals that the parallelism is between the phrase that starts with *what effects* and the one that starts with *how these*. Perhaps the parallelism becomes clear if we write the sentence like this:

It is hoped that the results obtained can be used to form predictions of
what effects similar additives will have on the mixtures
and
how these changes will affect the process.

We recognize that the preparatory phrase is too wordy, being redundant (results obtained) and containing an unnecessary verbal noun (predictions). Thus, we edit to

It is hoped that the results can be used to predict   (R1.29a)
what effects similar additives will have on the mixtures
and
how these changes will affect the process.

We make the parallelism more obvious by editing the last phrase to echo the first,

It is hoped that the results can be used to predict   (R1.29b)
what effects similar additives will have on the
mixtures and what effects these changes will have
on the process.

Parallelism leads readers to expect that sentences and phrases will adhere to certain structural forms. Such forms allow readers to concentrate on the message while ignoring grammar and syntax. When the parallelism extends over long phrases, or even sentences, then repetition can be used to reassure readers that the parallelism still applies, thereby allowing them to remain focussed on the message. So, don't lead readers to anticipate a particular parallel structure, and then frustrate them by not following through.

1.4 BE PRECISE

Precision means being specific rather than general and explicit rather than vague. In technical writing we can be precise not only through a proper use of words but also through a proper use of numbers. We perform experiments and calculations to obtain numbers, and numbers are primarily used to make comparisons. Thus, whenever numbers are available, we should use them to make comparisons quantitative.

Don't habitually write sentences like this,

> Method B performed better than method C. (E1.30)

Instead always consider whether a little numerical analysis will enable you to be quantitative; perhaps like this,

> Method B improved the efficiency by 20%, (R1.30)
> while method C improved it by only 10%.

The original (E1.30) expresses an opinion, but your idea of "better than" may be my idea of "about the same as." In contrast, the revision (R1.30) expresses a fact, within the uncertainties of the numbers. Similar vague generalities are listed, along with possible revisions, in Table 1.2. The revisions in the table are merely suggestions; the appropriate revision depends on context.

While qualitative statements and generalities are best avoided in the bodies of technical material, such statements are appropriate in summaries or conclusions. These are legitimate

Table 1.2
Common Generalities That Can Be Made More Precise.
The forms on the right are for illustration only. Context will dictate the particular form that you should use in place of any on the left.

Imprecise		More Precise
B is small	→	B is less than 1 cm.
the change in B was small	→	B increased by less than 1%
B is a good approximation to C	→	The sum of squares of deviations between B and C was less than 0.01.
little difference between B and C	→	B differs from C by 10 cm.
B compared favorably with C	→	B improved the efficiency by 10%, while C improved it by only 7%.
B had little effect on C	→	B never increased C by more than 5%.

because in the body of the work you have been quantitative; thus, in the body, you have either implicitly or explicitly defined what you mean by such general phrases as "better than."

Precision in language means proper choice of words and proper arrangement of the chosen words into sentences. In § 1.1 we noted that strong verbs generally produce more precise sentences than weak verbs. Here are two more ways to improve precision. One way is to be specific whenever possible. Don't write

The temperature was measured with a gage.   (E1.31)

when you mean

> The temperature was measured with a mercury (R1.31)
> thermometer.

We prefer (R1.31) over (E1.31) because by being specific we are more likely to create an image in the reader's mind. You have already had the lecture on the power of images (§ 1.1.1). Besides creating images, being specific increases your store of credibility with the reader; however if you are vague, your credibility decreases, and ultimately you may lose the reader's confidence.

A second way to improve precision is to choose the correct words for each sentence. Here are just a few examples from the many words that careless writers often confuse: accuracy–precision, affect–effect, alternate–alternative, cause–effect, correlate–predict, deduce–induce, demonstrate–prove, deviations–errors, principal–principle. To choose correctly, we must become sensitive to language and good usage.

1.5 DELETE UNNECESSARY WORDS

Effective writing proceeds by trial-and-error. We create a draft—a trial—and then we try to perfect the draft through a series of editorial iterations. By editing we hope to make our presentation logical and economical. Logical presentation is achieved mainly at the paragraph level, and so we discuss those problems in Chapter 3. However, economical presentation is achieved mainly at the sentence level, and so we discuss those problems here.

We emphasize that the economical use of words is accomplished, not in the drafting stage, but in the editorial stage. Don't censor usage while writing a first draft, else you suppress those creative impulses that often produce a happy turn of phrase and that occasionally generate new insight. When writers try to get it right the first time, they often succumb to mental constipation and writer's block. To avoid such problems, let yourself write a bad first draft, then improve it by conscientious editing.

Editing is motivated by an attitude of parsimony, just as parsimony motivates concise statements of scientific laws and promotes economical designs in engineering. A scientific equation contains no unnecessary terms and a manufacturing process involves no unnecessary raw materials; likewise, a coherent paragraph contains no unnecessary sentences and a strong sentence contains no superfluous words [5].

1.5.1 REMOVE REDUNDANCIES

First drafts are naturally infested with redundancies. The sin is not in writing them the first time, the sin occurs when we fail to delete them during editing. For example,

> The viscosity of the syrup was found to be a   (E1.32)
> function of the temperature of the syrup.

You know how to fix this. More insidious are redundancies that convey a false air of parallelism. Don't confuse the repetition in parallel structures with redundancies that add weight to a sentence without clarifying the message. Here is an example:

> Because the computer program was written   (E1.33)
> in machine language and could not be read
> to determine its validity, it was required to
> study the results of the program to determine
> their validity.

In this example the double use of "to determine validity" is not a parallelism, but a useless repetition. Remove one of them:

> Because the computer program was written   (R1.33)
> in machine language, its validity could be
> determined only by comparing its results to the
> solutions known to satisfy the following test problems.

1.5.2 DELETE UNNECESSARY QUALIFIERS

Unnecessary qualifiers pervade colloquial speech, but they should not appear in technical writing. Useless qualifiers can appear as phrases as well as single words. A common example is the prepositional phrase, such as in this sentence,

> Both of these problems are discussed in the (E1.34)
> next chapter.

Here the prepositional phrase can be reduced to its object,

> Both problems are discussed in the next chapter. (R1.34)

In some sentences, such as

> Many UFOs are red in color, spherical in shape, (E1.35)
> and metallic in nature.

the prepositional phrases can be completely eliminated,

> Many UFOs are red, spherical, and metallic. (R1.35)

Another common redundancy is the single word used for emphasis in colloquial speech; for example,

> To slow down the chemical reaction, remove heat. (E1.36)

But in writing, this kind of emphasis is misplaced, and the extra word should be deleted,

> To slow the chemical reaction, remove heat. (R1.36)

Other unnecessary qualifiers are listed in Table 1.3.

Table 1.3
Qualifiers in the Following Phrases (left)
Can Be Safely Deleted (right).

Less Economical		More Economical
cancel out	→	cancel
draw up into	→	draw into
made up of	→	made of (or made from)
migrate away from	→	migrate from
slow down	→	slow (or decelerate or retard)
speed up	→	speed (or accelerate)

1.5.3 REDUCE WORDY PHRASES TO ECONOMICAL FORMS

Besides redundancies and unnecessary qualifiers, many other colloquialisms and extraneous words enter our drafts. For example,

> The temperature was decreased to the level   (E1.37)
> at which the champagne froze.

Such verbiage must be removed during editing:

> The temperature was decreased until the   (R1.37)
> champagne froze.

More nonfunctional word-groups are listed in Table 1.4; pay particular attention to the phrases "in order to", "it should be noted that", and "on account of the fact that" which are ubiquitous but totally superfluous.

Table 1.4

Wordy Phrases (left) That Can Be Reduced
to More Economical Forms (right).

Less Economical		More Economical
all results presented in this study	→	all our results
another way this can be expressed is by saying that	→	in other words
avoid the possibility of	→	avoid
concerns the fact that	→	is that (or deals with)
data points taken	→	measured
doing this	→	this
due to the fact that	→	because
each of the	→	each
first of all	→	first
gives a visual indication	→	shows
has a higher degree of accuracy than	→	is more accurate than
in addition to	→	besides
increased to the level at which	→	increased until
in order that	→	so that
in order to	→	to
involves the use of	→	involves (or uses)
it is easy to	→	we can
it is possible to	→	we can
it is recommended by most authors that	→	most authors recommend that
it requires prior knowledge of	→	we must know

Table 1.4 (continued)

Less Economical		More Economical
it should be noted that	→	note that
it was assumed that	→	we assumed that
it was decided to drop	→	we eliminated
it was shown by them that	→	they showed that
negligibly small	→	negligible
on account of the fact that	→	because
over and above	→	greater than
provides a detailed account of	→	describes
reduced to the point at which	→	reduced until
reported in the literature by	→	reported by
should be equal to	→	should equal
this can be compensated for by	→	to compensate, we
this involves the use of	→	this uses
this was found to be	→	this was
this is an indication that	→	this shows that
to take into account	→	to account for
was able to	→	could
was measured experimentally	→	was measured
was observed to change	→	changed
was observed to vary	→	changed
wide range of	→	many
wide variety of	→	many
worked out solutions for	→	solved

1.6 SUMMARY

In this chapter we have brought to your attention certain rules of grammar and conventions of usage (syntax) that lead to clear and economical writing. In most instances we have cited the rule or convention, provided a rationale, and offered an example to illustrate how the rule or convention improves communication. But although we have touched on many aspects of writing, the points we have emphasized are but a subset from the larger body of rules of English grammar. Why all the rules? Many of the grammatical rules and syntactical conventions are arbitrary, so what purpose do they serve?

First, most rules and conventions codify what previous writers have learned as the best ways to write. Examples include the use of parallelism and the attention to linkage. By becoming explicitly aware of the things learned by others, we don't waste time reinventing the wheel.

Second, a commonly accepted set of rules and conventions serves as a background—a framework—for conveying messages. It is unimportant that some of the rules and conventions are arbitrary; what is important is that the rules and conventions are universally accepted. The situation is analogous to radio communications: in a radio transmission, the message is imposed on a carrier wave. But if I tune my radio receiver to a carrier frequency that differs from the frequency of your transmitter, then I miss your message. Similarly, in written work the message is superimposed on the background of good usage. But if you and I do not accept the same rules of usage—if we choose different backgrounds—then the message is corrupted or perhaps lost entirely.

Good usage remains in the background—it is inconspicuous. Effective writing never calls attention to itself; it never draws the reader's attention from what the message is to how the message is being conveyed. In radio communications, if the carrier intrudes, then the message is degraded or lost in noise. Any time we allow the background to intrude into the foreground, we jeopardize the effectiveness of the transmission.

Good usage is also economical—it conveys the intended message in a small number of words. But economical does not mean miserly; rather, economical usage strikes a balance between a profuse and a penurious use of words. When readers encounter profuse usage, they become jaded and inattentive; when they encounter penurious usage, they become perplexed and inattentive. But when our writing is balanced between these extremes—when readers are told enough, but not too much— then they are stimulated to appeal to their own experiences in decoding the message. It is this kind of active participation that most firmly holds a reader's interest

EXERCISES

1.1 Edit the following sentences to strengthen the verbs:
  (a) The temperature of the reactor has an effect on the speed of the reaction.
  (b) These assumptions are for the case when the flow is laminar.
  (c) There are two steps in deriving this equation.
  (d) The data were subjected to being divided into two groups.
  (e) With too few iterations, the algorithm is unable to converge to a solution.
  (f) The common idea behind these two methods is to split the disturbance term into two terms.

1.2 Edit the following by removing the verbal nouns:
  (a) These policies may contribute to the degradation in the morale of the workers.
  (b) These data were the result of much study and little experimentation.
  (c) The determination of the value may achieve optimization by proper calculation.
  (d) Is dilution the solution to pollution?

1.3 Edit the following to improve the use of modifiers:

(a) A stirred series-reaction batch reactor with temperature control was studied.

(b) The data set was scaled by a critical temperature to make the data points dimensionless.

(c) The experiment was extremely difficult to perform, but the results are very reliable.

(d) A criteria for reaching two-phase equilibria was studied.

(e) A nth-order term was added to the equation, to make it agree with the two maxima points.

1.4 Edit these to reduce, eliminate, or revise phrases:

(a) In order to test the theory, a wide range of values were measured experimentally.

(b) To understand why this is so, it should be noted that it was assumed that a steady-state was attained.

(c) The results were obtained from the apparatus by carefully removing the shield from the access port on the left side of the condenser.

(d) This section of the report provides a detailed account of how the numbers were calculated.

(e) The values reported here have a higher degree of accuracy on account of the fact that they were observed to change so slowly.

1.5 Write a complete step-by-step procedure for sharpening a pencil.

1.6 Write a complete step-by-step procedure for using a microwave oven to make a cup of instant coffee.

1.7 Articulate distinctions between members of each of the following pairs:

(a) bottle-jar	(f) formula-equation
(b) flotsam-jetsam	(g) virus-bacteria
(c) tube-hose	(h) theory-correlation
(d) fruit-vegetable	(i) measurement-experiment
(e) motor-engine	(j) science-engineering

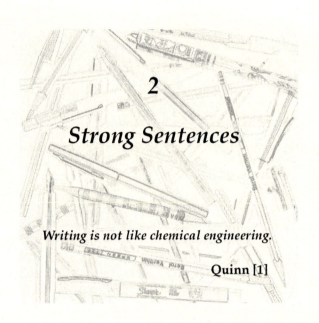

2

Strong Sentences

Writing is not like chemical engineering.

Quinn [1]

Since we aim to write not only correctly, but also effectively, we must learn how to combine words and phrases into strong sentences. To achieve strong sentences we must choose the voice of the verb correctly (§ 2.1), place important words at the points of emphasis in the sentence (§ 2.2), and ensure that sentence elements are clearly linked (§ 2.3).

2.1 ACTIVE VS PASSIVE

Recall that voice denotes the direction of the action. In the active voice the verb carries the action from the subject into the rest of the sentence; for example,

> The early bird ate the worm. (E2.1)

But in the passive voice the verb deflects the action back to the subject,

The worm was eaten by the early bird. (E2.2)

The active voice offers at least three advantages over the passive voice. First note that both voices invoke strong verbs, and recall from § 1.1 that strong verbs can suggest images. But images are stimulated more often by direct action than by indirect action. So to gain full benefit from a strong verb, use it in the active voice.

Second note that, in the active voice, the action is "natural" in the sense that it moves in the direction of our reading. But in the passive voice the action is artificial because the motion is opposed to the direction of reading. Consequently, compared to the passive voice, the active voice is more easily read and understood.

Third note that a sentence in the active voice requires fewer words than its counterpart in the passive voice. For example, in the passive voice, (E2.2) uses eight words; but to say exactly the same thing in the active voice, (E2.1) uses six words. The reduction is 25%, which would be significant if every sentence could be reduced by the same fraction. In general, sentences in the passive voice tend to be long and convoluted, while those in the active voice tend to be shorter, easier to read, and easier to understand.

The volume of technical information is increasing at an overwhelming rate. Two generations ago, scientists and engineers could build long careers on the knowledge gained in schools. No more. The half-life of technical knowledge is now no more than five years, in some fields it is less. Today's readers and writers cannot devote substantial time and mental effort to coding and decoding obstructive writing. The complexities of technical material are burden enough, without having those complexities compounded by an obscure writing style.

Why then has the passive voice come to dominate the literature of both science and engineering? The argument is that, by avoiding any explicit reference to the authors, the passive voice gives technical writing an air of objectivity. Thus we were taught to write sentences like this:

> It is not felt that the inclusion of another term (E2.3a)
> in the equation to account for this effect is needed.

Notice how the passive voice, verbal noun, prepositional phrases, and terminal verb all combine to make a sentence that is stilted and hard to grasp. But if (E2.3a) seems acceptable to you, try using the same structure with common nouns; for example,

> It is not felt that the inclusion of more ice in (E2.3b)
> the drink to account for the heat is needed.

Does this unambiguously and quickly convey information? Is (E2.3b) in any sense economical? One possible revision of (E2.3a) is

> In our opinion this effect does not justify adding (R2.3a)
> another term to the equation.

Another is

> In our opinion we do not need another term (R2.3b)
> in the equation.

Both revisions are straightforward and to the point. The choice between these two depends on context and on what we intend to emphasize—these issues will be addressed in § 2.2 and in Chapter 3.

But if we introduce personal pronouns such as *our* and *we*, don't we subvert disinterested objectivity? Not necessarily. Consider the following excerpt from an influential book on numerical methods (from *Numerical Recipes* [2], reprinted with permission from Cambridge University Press):

What we see is that least-squares fitting is a maximum likelihood estimation of the fitted parameters if the measurement errors are independent and normally distributed with constant standard deviation. Notice that we made no assumption about the linearity or nonlinearity of the model $y(x; a_1, ...)$ in its parameters $a_1 ... a_m$.

In these sentences *we* is used in two different ways. In the first sentence *we* broadly refers to authors and readers; such usage encourages readers to identify with the material and to participate in its development. But in the second sentence *we* refers just to the authors. Here both uses are unobtrusive and neither damages the credibility or objectivity of the authors; on the contrary, such usage signals the authors' confidence and authority in communicating the material.

In an earlier age, the advantages of the active voice were preserved by using the impersonal pronoun *one*. Thus the sentences in the above quotation would have started like this:

What one sees is that ...   and   Notice that one made no assumption ...

But this use of *one* is unfamiliar to the modern ear and would likely distract many readers. Moreover, in technical work, some readers would momentarily confuse the pronoun *one* with the number *one*. *One* has been replaced by *we* as an impersonal pronoun.

If you demur at using the active voice coupled with *we* unless sanctions are forthcoming from recognized authority, then demur no longer: Webster's Ninth New Collegiate Dictionary [3], we: ... *used by writers to keep an impersonal character;* American Heritage Dictionary of the English Language [4], we: ... *Used instead of I, especially by ... a writer wishing to maintain an impersonal tone;* Oxford English Dictionary [5]: we: ... *Used ... by a speaker or writer, in order to secure an impersonal style and tone, or to avoid the obtrusive repetition of 'I'.*

Are all authorities in agreement on this issue? Frankly no, they are not. W. H. Fowler, for one, refuses to accept *we* as an impersonal pronoun; rather, he encourages the modern preference for the bold use of *I* and *me* [6]. So if you feel uncomfortable using the first person plural, go ahead—be bold—use the first person singular. In fact, use whatever pronouns you like; I'm merely trying to convince you to use verbs in the active voice.

Now two cautions. First, avoid attaching *we* to statements of opinion; that is, don't write *we believe, we think*, or the like, unless it is clear that the *we* refers only to the authors. If the *we* in such forms can be interpreted as referring to authors and readers, then the writing may seem presumptuous or, worse, as an attempt to project attitudes onto the reader: you run the risk of antagonizing your readers.

Second, although we have emphasized use of the active voice, we cannot altogether abandon the passive voice. The active voice is not appropriate for every sentence; indeed, the passive voice plays a necessary role in linking sentences into coherent paragraphs. This use of the passive voice is addressed in § 3.2.1. The lesson of this section comes to this: make *proper* use of the passive voice.

2.2 EMPHASIS

In English we can change the meaning of a sentence by merely rearranging the words. More subtly, some rearrangements preserve the meaning but shift the emphasis. So the proper arrangement of words gives both the desired meaning and the desired emphasis. We first consider where the emphasis falls in a sentence (§ 2.2.1), then we consider how words should be arranged to take advantage of those points of emphasis (§ 2.2.2).

2.2.1 PLACE IMPORTANT WORDS AT POINTS OF EMPHASIS

In written material, where does the emphasis naturally lie? Let's consider two extremes: a short sentence and an extended piece of writing. For the short sentence, consider this:

They are here.   (E2.4)

This sentence often means that they have arrived, but it might also mean that they are in this location, rather than in some other location. One rearrangement of (E2.4) would yield,

Are they here?   (E2.5)

Obviously this has an altogether different meaning from (E2.4). Here's another rearrangement,

Here they are!   (E2.6)

which may mean, after much searching, I've finally found them.

In each of these three, where is the emphasis? If you read each aloud, where does the stress naturally fall? It falls at the beginning and again at the end:

They are **here**.   **Are** they **here**?   **Here** they **are**!

Beginnings and endings carry extra weight—first encounters and last encounters make memorable impressions; this seems to be true not only for sentences but also for paragraphs, sections, and chapters. Thus we should try to place our most important ideas at beginnings and endings.

For another example, consider a technical thesis, which is often organized like this:

Introduction, which motivates the study,
Literature Review, which tells what's been done before,

Procedure, which cites the experimental or computational methods used,

Results, which tells what data were obtained,

Discussion, which interprets the results,

Conclusion, which attaches meaning to the results by
placing them within the context of accepted knowledge.

Of these, the most important parts are the Introduction, which
tells why the work was done, and the Conclusion, which tells
how the results fit into a larger context. That is, in this standard
organization we place the most important parts at the beginning
and at the end. Similarly, in writing individual sentences, we
should use the natural points of stress to emphasize the important ideas.

It is not surprising that stress naturally falls at the beginning
of sentences: most sentences begin with their subjects, and the
subject is what a sentence is all about. But it may be less obvious
that stress also falls at the ends of most sentences. So give attention to endings. Aim to end sentences, not with prepositions,
adjectives, adverbs, passive verbs, or weak prepositional
phrases, but with strong parts of speech. You won't be able to do
this in every sentence, but you can do it for many. Make a special
effort at the end of the last sentence in a paragraph, for in bring-
ing to a close both a sentence and a group of related sentences,
the effect is amplified.

Let's consider some sample sentences. First,

Of these, Ockham's razor was the most important   (E2.7)
of them.

Since this sentence explicitly articulates what's most important,
emphasize that importance by putting the razor in its proper
place:

Of these, the most important was Ockham's razor.   (R2.7)

Another,

> Sunlight did influence several factors that may   (E2.8)
> affect employee performance directly or indirectly.

Do you sense waffling here—that the writer is ambivalent about the material? The arrangement of words influences how the reader perceives the author, and that perception determines whether the reader has confidence in what's written. To strengthen (E2.8), move those adverbs from the end,

> Sunlight did influence several factors that   (R2.8)
> may, either directly or indirectly, affect employee
> performance.

This revision conveys the attitude that it isn't so important whether the effect is direct or indirect; what's important is that there *does* seem to be an effect.

Here is a structure common to technical writing,

> The results were A and B for runs 1 and 2,   (E2.9)
> respectively.

The *respectively* is an unimportant deflating after-thought that draws our attention away from what is important: A and B. This structure is used to save words, but here are three reasons why its use is false economy. First, we can eliminate *respectively* and still avoid confusion by writing

> The results were A for run 1 and B for run 2.   (R2.9)

Note that (R2.9) has the same number of words as (E2.9): the original (E2.9) has not saved any words at all. Second, to decode the original (E2.9), the reader must pause and mentally match A to 1 and B to 2. In other words, the structure (E2.9) draws the reader's attention from *what* is being said to *how* it is being said. But in the revision (R2.9), the writer has already done the matching, so the revision is more readily assimilated than the original. Third, in writing the original and in proof-reading it, the writer must also perform the mental matching; in contrast, the revision is easier to write and proof. Thus by using (R2.9) the writer reduces the chances of inadvertently mismatching A with run 2 and B with run 1.

If you have assignments to make among triplets, the procedure is unchanged; instead of this,

$$\text{The results were A, B, and C for runs 1, 2,} \qquad \text{(E2.10)}$$
$$\text{and 3, respectively.}$$

you can use the same number of words to write this:

$$\text{The results were A for run 1, B for 2, and C for 3.} \qquad \text{(R2.10)}$$

In this revision the parallel pattern allows us to abbreviate *run 2* and *run 3* without loss of clarity. If you have more than three sets of assignments to make, consider using a table.

2.2.2 ARRANGE WORDS IN THEIR PROPER ORDER

We have seen that a sentence stresses its beginning and its ending, but how should words in between be ordered? What is the proper progression from start to finish? For a hint, look again at the standard organization of a thesis (§ 2.2.1). A thesis starts with a Literature Review, which contains *known* information, and ends with a Conclusion, which contains *new* information.

For another hint, consider this example:

$$\text{The following equation was derived in the} \qquad \text{(E2.11)}$$
$$\text{previous chapter.}$$

This sentence is weak because the emphasis is misplaced. Recall that the emphasis should fall on what's most important—either the point we are trying to make, or more often, whatever comes next. What comes next is important because it pushes us toward the point we are trying to make. Presumably what will follow (E2.11) is the equation itself—so that's what should be emphasized. Therefore "following equation" should end the sentence:

> In the previous chapter we derived the following   (R2.11)
> equation.

The sentence (E2.11) should bridge from "previous chapter" to "following equation", but it has inverted the natural order by mentioning what comes next *before* mentioning what came earlier. This unnatural order is corrected in the revision (R2.11).

In the revision (R2.11) and in the organization of a thesis we see that the proper order is *from* previous information *to* new information. Again we extend this observation to all writing, to theses, reports, papers, chapters, sections, paragraphs, and sentences. In every case the appropriate order of presentation is this:

$$\text{Old} \;\rightarrow\; \text{New}$$

Always start with something you can reasonably expect your readers to know: a generality or something that is common knowledge or something you've just told them.

The rule old → new can guide us through many editorial dilemmas. For example, by applying the rule during editing, we can improve such familiar patterns as these three:

Transitional Sentences. These sentences explicitly connect old material to new; (E2.11) is an example. Similar structures occur routinely, often in one of the following forms:

> the following assumptions
> the following chapter
> the following derivation
> the following equation

the following procedure
the following steps

Such phrases should occur at the ends of transitional sentences.

Dates at ends of sentences. Sometimes old information is explicitly dated, so we immediately know to move it from the end of a sentence.

> The zipper has become the common fastener for   (E2.12)
> clothing since its invention by Gideon Sundback
> in 1913.

Certainly 1913 is old and unless the author is about to discuss the year 1913, the sentence would be better written like this:

> Invented in 1913 by Gideon Sundback, the   (R2.12)
> zipper has become the common fastener for
> clothing.

This pattern also occurs in more subtle forms; for example,

> Chemical reactions have been known to be   (E2.13)
> temperature dependent for a long time.

Note how the emphasis at the end accentuates the weak linkage: is the prepositional phrase modifying *known* or *dependent*? Perhaps reactions have been dependent for a while, but not always? Presumably temperature should be emphasized, so

> Chemical reactions have long been known to   (R2.13)
> depend on temperature.

Terminal *this*-phrase. Watch for sentences that end with *this such-and-such.* Often, *this such-and-such* was just discussed in the previous sentence and so it is now old information. When this occurs, recast the sentence to place that old information at the beginning. For example,

No meteor showers were observed for this reason.   (E2.14)

is better phrased as

For this reason no meteor showers were observed.   (R2.14a)

or

For this reason we observed no meteor showers.   (R2.14b)

The choice is whether the writer wants to emphasize "observed" or "meteors". This lesson has also been tacitly illustrated in the earlier examples (E1.6), (E2.3a), and their revisions.

2.3 LINKAGE

If word order were used solely to achieve emphasis, then writing would not be so difficult. But in addition to emphasis, word order also establishes linkage between sentence elements. *Linkage* refers to those connections that help the reader understand the message intended by the writer [7]. Examples of linkage include the connections between a verb and its subject, between a modifier and the word modified, and between a pronoun and its antecedent. The key to linkage is proximity: to convey the intended linkage between elements, keep those elements close together.

Editing becomes challenging when the word order required for proper emphasis conflicts with the order required for coherent linkage. Often these conflicts can be resolved by changing the voice of the verb, either from active to passive or from passive to active. In other sentences conflicts occur because we are trying to load too many ideas into a single sentence; then we should break the overloaded structure into two or more parts. But in editing any sentence, no matter what its problems, we should strive first for proper linkage—achieving coherent linkage takes precedence over all other aspects of style.

2.3.1 KEEP THE VERB CLOSE TO ITS SUBJECT

In § 1.2.2 we discussed how apparent conflicts in number can be avoided by keeping the verb close to its subject. But agreement in number is only one aspect of proper linkage; in fact, all aspects are strengthened when the verb closely follows its subject. The relation between subject and verb is a particularly important one and in most sentences that relation should be established quickly. If many words separate the verb from its subject, then tension is created in the reader. In the hurry to find the verb and relieve the tension, the reader may skim over intervening words and miss part of the message. Moreover, such separations often defeat the natural points of emphasis, making the beginning or ending of the sentence weak and unsatisfying.

Consider the following example, which we have seen before,

> The determination of the effect of a structural (E2.15) breakdown during the low frequency test on the response curve of the high frequency test is shown in Figure 7.

In § 1.1.3.4 we discussed how such strings of prepositional phrases reduce coherence. But in this example coherence is also weakened because a verbal noun serves as the subject and because the subject is poorly linked to its verb. In the revision (R1.16) we strengthened the sentence by making "Figure 7" the subject and by placing the subject immediately before the verb—"Figure 7 shows...". But if the sentence (E2.15) is intended to introduce the figure, then a better revision is

> We determined how a structural breakdown (R2.15) during the low frequency test affects the response curve of the high frequency test; the result is shown in Figure 7.

In isolation, the revisions (R1.16) and (R2.15) are equally strong; the choice depends on context.

When nonrestrictive phrases separate a verb from its subject, as in (E2.15), then a simple revision will usually leave the sentence in a stronger form. But when the subject and verb are separated by a restrictive clause, then a simple revision may be difficult or impossible to find. In such cases we need to strengthen the linkage between subject and verb while maintaining the linkage between subject and clause. For example,

> A person who performs satisfactorily when (E2.16)
> exposed to an unfamiliar and stressful situation
> and who makes the performance look easy is
> generally referred to as a professional.

Such dilemmas can often be resolved by repeating the subject immediately before the verb:

> If a person performs satisfactorily and effort- (R2.16)
> lessly when exposed to an unfamiliar and
> stressful situation, then that person is generally
> called a professional.

When editing, watch for *terminal verbs*—verbs separated from their subjects and placed at the ends of sentences. By occupying a point of emphasis, a terminal verb tends to amplify the underlying weakness of the sentence. Such sentences often take the form subject-clause-verb or subject-phrase-verb. Thus,

> The effect of ripe banana incorporation on the (E2.17)
> speed of learning and resulting memory
> retention is shown.

Here the terminal verb amplifies the weakness caused by the verbal noun, sequence of prepositional phrases, weak subject-verb linkage, and unnecessary words. By now you should know how to fix such a sentence:

> We show how ripe bananas affect learning (R2.17)
> and memory.

An exception occurs if you manage to end a sentence with a verb strongly linked to its subject, for then you may have achieved a sentence having special strength. But as with all rhetorical devices that add emphasis, this device should rarely be used.

2.3.2 PLACE PHRASES AND CLAUSES CORRECTLY

We do not recite the numerous ways that subordinate phrases and clauses can be misplaced, thereby creating ambiguous or unintended linkage. However of those many ways, two are particularly prevalent and we use them to illustrate the entire class of misplacements. Both examples involve phrases or clauses applied to the subject.

(a) Phrases and clauses placed in the predicate should not modify the subject. For example,

> Equations have now been presented that apply to both models. (E2.18)

Here the restrictive clause (*that...*) is poorly linked to the subject. This is another example of the conflict that can arise when we try to link a subject to its verb and also to a subordinate clause. In this example the problem is ultimately caused by the writer's use of the passive voice, and so the easiest way to resolve the conflict is to change to the active voice:

> We have now presented equations that apply to both models. (R2.18)

(b) Introductory phrases and clauses generally refer to the subject. As a violation of this rule, consider the following:

> Before proving this claim, a short review of previous efforts will be presented. (E2.19)

In this sentence the poor linkage produces ambiguity: Is the short review going to prove the claim or not? This problem can also be attributed to the use of the passive voice, so removing the passive voice removes the ambiguity:

> Before proving this claim, we review previous (R2.19)
> efforts.

However, an introductory phrase need not refer to the subject if the phrase is of a general nature (it does not imply action on the part of the subject), and if it serves to link the sentence to an earlier word, phrase, or sentence. For example,

> In spite of these many attempts, all previous (E2.20)
> proofs are wrong.

Further, if the introductory phrase contains a noun (or pronoun) acting as the subject of a verb participle, then the phrase is independent, and it need not refer to the subject of the sentence. Thus, the following sentence is grammatically correct,

> Before we prove this claim, a short review (E2.21)
> of previous efforts will be presented.

2.3.3 KEEP PRONOUNS CLEARLY LINKED TO ANTECEDENTS

One symptom of careless writing is a consistent decoupling of pronouns from their antecedents; the underlying disease is inadequate editing. In technical writing the most-often used pronouns are *it*, *that*, and *which*—three little words that, misused, can cause great confusion. Here is an example:

> These differences indicate that it was the (E2.22)
> inhomogeneity developed in the sample and
> not its composition which accounts for its
> peculiar behavior.

This sentence illustrates two misuses. First, the antecedent of *which* is not immediately clear: is it *composition*, or *sample*, or *inhomogeneity*? Context—not sentence structure—suggests that the antecedent is *inhomogeneity*. Second, *it* is used in two different ways. In the first use *it* serves as the indefinite pronoun, but in the two subsequent uses *it* refers to *sample*. Within a single sentence such double meanings should be avoided.

Unclear antecedents may signal fundamental structural flaws that cannot be corrected by simply reducing the distance between the pronoun and its antecedent. In (E2.22) the fundamental problem is misplaced emphasis; therefore in editing (E2.22), we aim to remove the ambiguities by emphasizing what is most important. Example (E2.22) ends by emphasizing *peculiar behavior*, but the content of (E2.22) suggests that the most important idea is, in fact, the inhomogeneity, because the inhomogeneity explains the peculiar behavior. Thus we write,

> These differences indicate that the peculiar (R2.22)
> behavior was caused, not by the composition
> of the sample, but by its inhomogeneity.

By moving the most important word to a point of emphasis, we solve much of the problem. Finally note that in (R2.22) the phrase *of the sample* has been placed to modify *composition*, rather than *behavior*. By this placement, the antecedent (*sample*) becomes the last noun to appear before the single occurrence of the pronoun *its*: we have used proximity to achieve linkage.

2.4 SUMMARY

Engineering design, scientific research, composing music, and technical writing are creative activities, and all creative acts proceed by trial and error [8]. In writing, the trial-and-error process occurs during editing not during drafting, and in editing our intention is to improve the writing by eliminating flaws.

To be effective editors we must be able to identify flaws, understand why the flaws detract from coherence, and know how the flaws can be corrected.

In Chapters 1 and 2 we have emphasized precision and linkage: precision in the choice of words to use and linkage in the placement of words in sentences. But precision and linkage are only necessary for coherent communication, they are not sufficient. The third requirement is that the writing must connect to the experience and knowledge of the reader. This is not only a matter of jargon, but more subtly, an expectation that the reader is capable of reading between the lines.

Since the writer is in control of the communication, the writer has the responsibility of crafting the message so that readers can relate to the message and understand it. This is probably best accomplished if you write with a particular individual in mind. Don't write abstractly—put a name and a face to a representative reader.

Ultimately, the whole business comes to this: help the reader get the message. Whenever the writing distracts the reader from the message, then the writing is wasted. Such writing is neither coherent nor economical.

EXERCISES

2.1 Revise the following sentences from passive to active voice:
   (a) The data were measured by a technician.
   (b) These conclusions are supported by the data.
   (c) The results are shown in Figure 2.
   (d) Although the procedure was wrong, accurate and precise results were obtained.
   (e) The normal boiling point was reached in the apparatus, but boiling did not occur.

2.2 Revise the following sentences from active to passive voice:
   (a) The next section of the report contains the protocol.

(b) The technician recorded the values in the lab notebook.

(c) This equation shows the relation between the two variables.

(d) These error bars indicate relative error in the measurements.

(e) The computer failed to complete the calculations.

2.3 Consider this sentence:

> Sunlight influences several factors that can affect employee performance.

(a) Revise this sentence so the emphasis is on "factors."

(b) Revise it so the emphasis is on "employees."

(c) Revise is so the emphasis is on "performance."

2.4 Consider this sentence:

> Procedures often include schematic diagrams of equipment.

(a) Revise this sentence so the emphasis is on "diagrams."

(b) Revise it so the emphasis is on "equipment."

2.5 Edit the following sentences so that verbs are adjacent to their subjects:

(a) A set of steps that are to be repeated should be grouped into a single module.

(b) The following values for pressure at selected temperatures were recorded from the experiment.

(c) Procedures for start-up and shut-down of equipment must be followed carefully.

(d) Reliable values for an oscillating variable can be obtained by measuring at or below the Nyquist sampling frequency.

(e) As a check on the procedure, calculations that convert raw data into desired quantities should be performed while the experiment is in progress.

2.6 Edit the following sentence to improve linkage; you may want to divide it into two or more sentences.

> One way to obtain knowledge about system dynamics for which only observable signals are available is to use a flexible model that will imitate the manufacturing plant by changing its parameters to match the observable plant's output signal when driven by the same input.

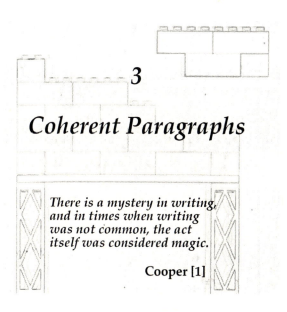

3

Coherent Paragraphs

There is a mystery in writing, and in times when writing was not common, the act itself was considered magic.

Cooper [1]

If we imagine sentences are like bricks, then paragraphs are the courses of brick that we assemble into a written structure. The resilience of a brick structure depends not only on the integrity and placement of individual bricks, but also on the mortar that binds one brick to another. Likewise the coherence of a paragraph depends not only on the strength and placement of individual sentences, but also on the linkage that binds one sentence to another. In coherent paragraphs, sentences are clearly linked.

There are many ways of organizing sentences into effective paragraphs, and consequently paragraphs could be divided into numerous kinds or classes. But such an extensive classification would not be particularly instructive. However, it may be instructive to look at the structures of some elementary paragraphs; so, in this chapter a few simple structures are used to show how linkage contributes to coherent paragraphs.

Simple paragraphs can be divided into two principal types: those having sentence-to-theme linkage and those having sentence-to-sentence linkage. In sentence-to-theme linkage each sentence is linked directly to the theme or to some other point of focus. In sentence-to-sentence linkage the sentences are linked to one another. These are certainly not the only ways to link sentences into coherent paragraphs, but these are enough to provide grounds for discussion.

In this chapter we are not advocating that paragraphs should be restricted to a few simple forms. Doing so would limit our writing to a meager range of expression. Instead, we are merely trying to use simple structures to illustrate the importance of linkage. If we are aware that linkage promotes coherence and if we have some simple model paragraphs to guide our thinking, then we have some ideas about how to start editing our own writing. Our editing skills can then be improved with practice.

3.1 SENTENCE-TO-THEME LINKAGE

In simple sentence-to-theme linkage, the sentences in a paragraph are explicitly connected to the theme. In more advanced forms the connection may not be directly to the theme, but to some other focal point that serves to keep the reader oriented towards the writer's point of emphasis. In many paragraphs the linkage may be primarily sentence-to-theme, with sentence-to-sentence linkage serving a secondary role. Here we discuss three kinds of paragraphs having sentence-to-theme linkage: thematic paragraphs, radial paragraphs, and polyphonic paragraphs.

3.1.1 THEMATIC PARAGRAPHS

In a paragraph all sentences should develop or expound on a single object or idea. If that object or idea is placed at the start of every sentence, either as the subject or as a noun in an introductory phrase, then we have a *thematic paragraph*. The repetition forces every sentence to be explicitly linked to the theme. Here is a sample thematic paragraph composed of six sentences, each having *water* (or its surrogate *it*) as the subject,

> Water is a perfect medium for such processes as the transport of nutrients into cells and the carving of landscapes by flushing minerals out of rocks. Water appears to be essential for life, since it can provide a fluid environment within cells through which other molecules can migrate. Water can transport molecules up to cells, give them mobility within cells, and transport molecules away from cells to other locations. It can transport organic molecules like glucose and the ions of such elements as sodium, potassium, and calcium that are so essential to an organism's functioning. Moreover, water, when it is a liquid, can do all this at body temperature. Fortunately, it cannot dissolve the calcium phosphate of our bones, so that our skeletons do not dissolve in our own fluids and we do not wilt. (P. W. Atkins, *Molecules* [2]; reprinted with permission from P. W. Atkins.)

The thematic paragraph is often used to present a series of complex, but loosely connected, ideas. Recall that our guiding principle is *old* → *new*. When many sentences contain new, loosely connected information, then a simple way to satisfy *old* → *new* is to repeat the theme at the start of each sentence. By renaming the object that is common to loosely connected ideas, we keep the reader focussed on the main point of emphasis.

Consider this poorly linked paragraph:

> If algorithm 1 searches long enough, it will eventually converge to a solution. However, when the algorithm reaches the neighborhood of a solution, it fails to converge quickly. Therefore algorithm 2 was actually used to find the solution once the neighborhood was identified by algorithm 1.

The first two sentences both start by referring to algorithm 1, but the linkage is disrupted in the third sentence, which abruptly starts with new information (algorithm 2). By recasting the third sentence to conform to our rule old → new, we improve the linkage and create a thematic paragraph,

> If algorithm 1 searches long enough, it will eventually converge to a solution. However, when the algorithm reaches the neighborhood of a solution, it fails to converge quickly. Therefore, once algorithm 1 has identified the neighborhood, we replace algorithm 1 with algorithm 2 to find the solution.

Perhaps you have been guided by the notion that only lazy writers pen paragraphs in which each sentence starts with the same subject or same word. Perhaps you have the idea that such a paragraph signals a lack of creativity and makes monotonous reading. Perhaps your observations are valid, sometimes, but often they are not. The thematic paragraph provides a simple but effective way to establish linkage, to keep verbs close to their subjects, and to use predicates to develop the theme. In those thematic paragraphs in which the subject is the repeated object, importance shifts to the predicates—to the ends of the sentences. In such paragraphs the predicates can be used to introduce and develop ideas in ways that are both original and interesting.

3.1.2 RADIAL PARAGRAPHS

Another example of sentence-to-theme linkage is what we call a *radial paragraph*. In the radial form, the theme is stated in the first sentence, and subsequent sentences develop the theme, one aspect after another. Often, the theme constitutes a category, and the paragraph discusses members of the category. In other words, the first sentence identifies the hub of a wheel, and subsequent sentences trace out the spokes. This structure is common in technical writing; here's an example,

> In science and engineering, *energy* proves to be a useful bookkeeping quantity. *Kinetic energy* is associated with the velocity of an object relative to a space-fixed reference frame. Gravitational *potential energy* arises when an object is located in the gravitational field of another object. *Elastic strain energy* is the potential energy associated with the bending of a bow and the stretching of a spring. Other potential energies can occur when an object is placed in magnetic and electrical fields. (paraphrased from Fenn [3])

A radial paragraph is similar to a thematic paragraph, but a thematic paragraph usually cites attributes of a single object, while a radial paragraph usually cites members of a set. In a thematic paragraph the sentences are explicitly linked by renaming the object of interest. In a radial paragraph the sentences are linked through membership in a category; the linkage may be explicit or implicit.

The example offered above is typical of radial paragraphs, but in addition, the radial form can be used in subtle ways to sustain emphasis and preserve coherence. Consider this sample:

> To plumb the depth of our ignorance, consider that there are millions of insect species still unstudied, most or all of which harbor specialized bacteria. There are millions of other invertebrate species, from corals to crustaceans to starfish, in similar state. Consider that each bacterial type, each species if we employ the DNA-matching rule, can utilize at most a hundred carbon sources, such as different sugars or fatty acids. Most can in fact metabolize only one to several such compounds. Consider further that bacteria can evolve rapidly to exploit these resources. Different strains and even species readily exchange genes, especially during periods

of food shortage and other forms of environmental stress. Their generations are short, allowing natural selection to act on new assortments of genes within days or even hours, shifting the heredity this way or that, perhaps creating new species. (E. O. Wilson, *The Diversity of Life* [4]; reprinted with permission from E. O. Wilson.)

The phrase *consider that*, stated in the first sentence and repeated in the third and fifth sentences, serves to identify three spokes radiating from the hub of our ignorance. This repeated phrase links the sentences to the theme and guides the reader from one spoke of the wheel to the next. These sentences establish the primary linkage of the paragraph. Details about each spoke are provided by the other sentences. That is, the other sentences do not link directly to the theme; instead, each links to one of the spokes. These two structural devices may perhaps be clarified by the following diagram,

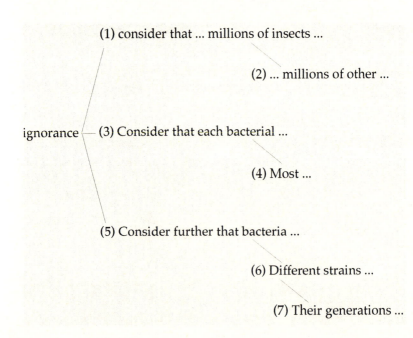

(1) consider that ... millions of insects ...

(2) ... millions of other ...

ignorance — (3) Consider that each bacterial ...

(4) Most ...

(5) Consider further that bacteria ...

(6) Different strains ...

(7) Their generations ...

In the diagram the numerals identify the serial position of each sentence in the paragraph, and the lines connect linking words. The diagram shows how the first, third, and fifth sentences link to the idea of ignorance, while the second, fourth, sixth, and seventh sentences link to earlier sentences. With the diagram we can see that Wilson's paragraph is not a simple structure; it is a compound paragraph in which the primary structural feature is sentence-to-theme linkage. But that primary structure is reinforced by secondary linkage which is sentence-to-sentence.

The lesson is not that you should emulate this structure; rather, the point is that, in such involved structures, coherence is preserved by strong linkage among sentences. So during editing, if you find a complex paragraph, look for ways to help guide the reader by emphasizing the linkage.

3.1.3 POLYPHONIC PARAGRAPHS

We now consider the extent to which a single paragraph can be used to discuss *two* central ideas. This may be desirable when we have two objects to compare or contrast. Actually, making comparisons—citing similarities—poses no particular difficulty: we merely combine the two objects into a single entity, and then recite their common attributes. The paragraph could easily take the thematic form.

But making contrasts—citing differences—is more problematic because each member of the pair must be linked to the appropriate attributes. To make this linkage coherent, we often make heavy use of repetition and parallelism, and we must resolve the conflicting demands of emphasis, logical order, and clarity. One effective structure occurs by organizing the paragraph so that the contrast is presented in an alternating fashion, phrase by phrase or sentence by sentence. This structure we call a *polyphonic form*; here is an example:

A piano and a harpsichord are both sounded by striking keys, but the two differ in how they make sound. A piano sounds by hitting strings with hammers, while a harpsichord sounds by plucking strings with plectra. With a piano we can control the volume of sound by changing the force applied to the keys, but with a harpsichord we have no such control because each string is plucked with the same intensity, no matter how hard the keys are struck. Further, the hammers on a piano are fitted with dampers that control the duration over which each note sounds. But the plectra on a harpsichord have no dampers, so each note sounds for nearly the same length of time. Consequently, a piano offers a wide expressive range that can be explored through large dramatic changes or through subtle shifts in shading. In contrast, a harpsichord offers only a limited range for expression.

This example is typical of polyphonic paragraphs: the first sentence identifies the two items to be compared, the next two sentences contrast phrase-by-phrase, building to longer phrases, then the last two sentences contrast sentence-by-sentence. Linkage is ensured by repeatedly referring to the two things being compared. Repetition is also used to reinforce the structure itself: pairs of phrases and sentences in each contrast are written in parallel forms.

3.2 SENTENCE-TO-SENTENCE LINKAGE

In a sentence-to-theme paragraph, each sentence is directly linked to a central idea, but in other paragraphs the sentences may link directly to one another; we call this *sentence-to-sentence* linkage. Sentence-to-sentence paragraphs are more common than those having sentence-to-theme linkage, but they are more difficult to write. In sentence-to-theme paragraphs linkage is communicated by repetition, but in sentence-to-sentence paragraphs linkage is communicated by proximity. The challenge is to keep linking words close together, even though they reside in different sentences. To meet the challenge of proximity, we employ a mix of active and passive voices. So in the sections that follow, we first show how the passive voice is properly used to link sentences into coherent paragraphs (§ 3.2.1). Then we introduce two kinds of paragraphs having sentence-to-sentence linkage: linear paragraphs (§ 3.2.2) and procedural paragraphs (§ 3.2.3).

3.2.1 PROPER USE OF THE PASSIVE VOICE

In § 2.1 we encouraged use of the active voice; to recall the issue, here is a paragraph in which all sentences are in the passive voice.

> The freezing point of water can be changed by adding salt. The size of the change can be determined from Figure 10, in which freezing points are plotted against salt concentration. For example, when the solution is 5% salt, the freezing point is lowered to $-3°C$. Thus salt is used to inhibit icing on wintry roads and to promote lower temperatures when making homemade ice cream.

We recognize that the passive verbs make this paragraph wordy, and although the linkage is linear, the linkage is weak because several linking words are widely separated. To show the linkage, we write the paragraph in a skeletal form:

(1) ... can be changed by adding salt. (2) The size of the change ...

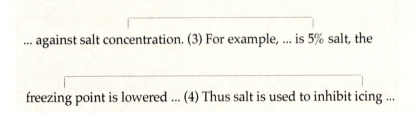

... against salt concentration. (3) For example, ... is 5% salt, the

freezing point is lowered ... (4) Thus salt is used to inhibit icing ...

We have placed a serial number at the start of each sentence and used horizontal lines to indicate linkage. When a line crosses a period, then the two sentences are linked. Long lines indicate weak links.

If we rewrite all sentences in the active voice, we reduce the number of words so the paragraph reads more briskly,

> The freezing point of water changes on adding salt. Figure 10, which plots freezing points against salt concentration, shows the size of the change. For example, when the concentration is 5% salt, the solution freezes at −3°C. Thus salt inhibits icing on wintry roads and promotes lower temperatures when making homemade ice cream.

But the paragraph is disjointed and the linkage unimproved,

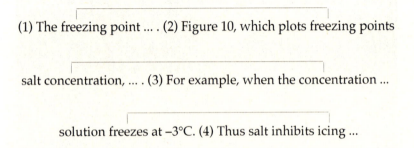

(1) The freezing point .... . (2) Figure 10, which plots freezing points

salt concentration, ... (3) For example, when the concentration ...

solution freezes at −3°C. (4) Thus salt inhibits icing ...

By writing every sentence in the same voice—active or passive—we may create a poorly linked paragraph. So in general, use the active voice whenever possible, but use the passive voice to maintain coherent linkage. Thus,

> When we add salt to water, the freezing point changes. The size of the change can be found from a plot of freezing point against salt concentration, as in Figure 10. For example, the figure shows that freezing occurs at −3°C when the concentration is 5% salt. Thus salt is used to inhibit icing on wintry roads and to promote lower temperatures when making homemade ice cream.

In this version the sentences alternate between active and passive; the first and third sentences are in the active voice, while the second and fourth are passive. As a result, the sentences are tightly linked:

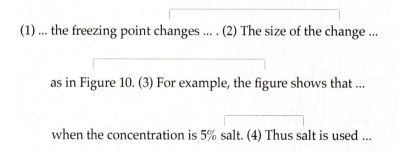

(1) ... the freezing point changes ... . (2) The size of the change ...

as in Figure 10. (3) For example, the figure shows that ...

when the concentration is 5% salt. (4) Thus salt is used ...

We should not eliminate the passive voice from our writing, but we should relegate it to its proper role—to link sentences into coherent paragraphs.

3.2.2 LINEAR PARAGRAPHS

When we explicitly link each sentence to its two neighboring sentences, we create a *linear paragraph.* The linkage is strictly linear when the end of each sentence explicitly connects to the beginning of the next sentence. Here is a strictly linear paragraph,

> It is not only large computers that are cause for concern, and some critics have expressed the fear that a greater danger lies in the growing use of microcomputers. Since these machines and a plethora of software for them are so readily available and so inexpensive, there is concern that engineers will take on jobs that are at best on the fringes of their expertise. And being inexperienced in an area, they are less likely to be critical of a computer-generated design that would make no sense to an older engineer who would have developed a feel for the structure through the many calculations he had performed on his slide rule. (H. Petroski, *To Engineer is Human* [5]; reprinted with permission from H. Petroski.)

In this paragraph the end of the first sentence is explicitly linked to the start of the second, just as the end of the second is linked to the start of the third. To show that linkage, we rewrite the paragraph in a skeletal form,

(1) ... a greater danger lies in the ...

use of microcomputers. (2) Since these machines ...

are so readily available ... engineers will take on jobs ...

on the fringes of their expertise. (3) And being inexperienced ...

they are less likely to be critical ...

Recall that the lines indicate linkage; when a line can be drawn across each period without crossing any other line, then the linkage is linear. If two lines cross one another, then one link remains unresolved while a second has been started. Such double linkages must be used with care, else they will weaken rather than strengthen the paragraph.

Few paragraphs have the end of each sentence explicitly linked to the beginning of the next sentence. But linear connections can be achieved in other ways; for example,

> In the previous chapter we found that everything is a combination of atomic nuclei and their electrons. The properties of all things result from an interplay of various electron patterns and their combinations. Electrons assume particular wave patterns when they assemble around atomic nuclei; they combine to form atoms and the atoms combine to form molecules. These combinations of electron patterns are responsible for the properties of all materials and make each substance unique.

The first sentence establishes linkage by referring to old information presented in the previous chapter. Further, these four sentences are individually strong: each verb is near its subject, the passive voice is not used, pronouns are clearly linked to their antecedents, etc. The skeletal form of this paragraph looks like this:

(1) ... we found ... that

everything ... is a combination of ... electrons. (2) ... all things ...

electron patterns ... . (3) Electrons assume particular ...

wave patterns ... . (4) These ... patterns ... make each substance ...

In this paragraph the first sentence is linked to the second in two ways: *everything* → *all things* at the start of each sentence, and *electrons* → *electron patterns* at the ends. Because of this double linkage, the paragraph is not strictly linear. But linearity does occur between sentences 2 and 3 and between 3 and 4. Thus, *electron patterns* at the end of 2 links to *electrons* at the start of 3, and *patterns* in 3 links to *patterns* at the start of 4.

This paragraph also contains two other connections that are somewhat subtle. First, in sentence 3 the phrase after the semicolon cites examples of wave patterns, so the entire phrase links to the first part of sentence 3 and to *patterns* at the start of sentence 4. Second, the paragraph ends with a subtle linking closure in which *each substance*, at the end of the paragraph, refers back to *everything*, which appeared in the first sentence.

We now turn to the editing that leads to a linear paragraph. To have an example, we use the same paragraph that we criticized in § 3.1.1,

> If algorithm 1 searches long enough, it will eventually converge to a solution. However, when the algorithm reaches the neighborhood of a solution, it fails to converge quickly. Therefore algorithm 2 was actually used to find the solution once the neighborhood was identified by algorithm 1.

In § 3.1.1 we edited this example into a thematic paragraph; we could also recast the second and third sentences to obtain a linear development. Thus,

> If algorithm 1 searches long enough, it will eventually converge to a solution. However, near a solution the algorithm fails to converge quickly. To avoid slow convergence, we used algorithm 1 to find the neighborhood of the solution, and then we used algorithm 2 to find the exact solution.

The skeletal form shows the linear structure,

(1) ... algorithm 1 ... converge to a solution. (2) ... solution ...

fails to converge ... . (3) To avoid slow convergence, ...

Note that all three sentences are written in the active voice. To use the active voice in the third sentence and to keep that sentence connected to the rest of the paragraph, we established linkage by placing a verbal noun in an introductory phrase (*converge → convergence*). This illustrates one proper use of verbal nouns; that is, when used carefully, verbal nouns can help maintain linkage without disrupting emphasis.

3.2.3 PROCEDURAL PARAGRAPHS

If we generalize the linear paragraph to give a step-by-step description of a process or behavior, then we create a *procedural paragraph*. But although a procedural paragraph can be viewed as an outgrowth of a linear paragraph, in a procedural paragraph the sentence linkage need not be linear. In fact the linkage may not even be totally explicit because the proper arrangement of sentences is imposed by the logical or temporal order of the process being described. However, explicit linkage is more coherent than implicit linkage, and many times implicit linkage can be made explicit by careful editing.

As an example of a procedural paragraph, consider the following excerpt, which describes part of the injection molding process for making certain plastic parts from the polymer acrylonitrile butadiene styrene:

When the "curing" of the bricks is finished, the mold automatically opens, and a robot arm reaches down to grab the length of excess plastic that has been extruded. The bricks fall into a cardboard box below, and the robot tosses the extra plastic, called the runner, into a bin, from which it is shunted to a hopper and recycled—the molding process wastes no plastic. Every few seconds, the box under each machine begins to rock back and forth as an automatic agitator shakes it so that the bricks will settle evenly. At any given moment, dozens of these agitators may be at work, tossing thousands of **LEGO** bricks and creating an unearthly rustling sound. The molding machines count the number of pieces they produce, and when a certain point is reached the machine knows that the box is full. Automatically, the full box is shunted aside and an empty box slides into its place. (H. Wiencek, *The World of LEGO® Toys* [6]; reprinted with permission from Harry N. Abrams, Inc.)

Note how this paragraph emphasizes the plastic bricks: every sentence, except the last, ends with a reference to the plastic or the bricks (or the box full of plastic bricks). The paragraph avoids verbal nouns and creates a sense of action by using many strong verbs: opens, reaches, extruded, fall, tosses, shunted, shakes, count, and slides.

In this paragraph the linkage is largely explicit, though in many procedural paragraphs some linkage can remain implicit. Some implicit linkage may not harm coherence because the sentences are linked through the order in which the procedure must be performed. However, when all linkage is implicit, the paragraph tends to be disjointed and may incur ambiguities; for example,

The gravimetric analysis was performed by the following procedure. First, a 200-ml sample was drawn from the suspension. This sample was centrifuged for 30 minutes, and the supernatant was decanted. Then the residue was suspended in distilled water and again centrifuged for 30 minutes. After decanting this supernatant, the residue was dried at 110°C for 12 hours and then weighed.

By overusing the passive voice, the writer has left unclear just who performed the analysis, the writer or an analytical lab? Moreover, without explicit linkage, the paragraph reads as a series of disconnected sentences.

By carefully mixing the active and passive voice and reordering some words, we can achieve explicit linkage:

We analyzed the suspension gravimetrically using the following procedure. From the suspension we drew a 200-ml sample. This sample was centrifuged for 30 minutes, and the supernatant was decanted, leaving a residue. This residue was then suspended in distilled water, creating a new mixture. The new mixture was centrifuged for another 30 minutes, the supernatant again decanted, and the new residue dried at 110°C for 12 hours. Then the residue was weighed.

In fact the linkage is completely linear,

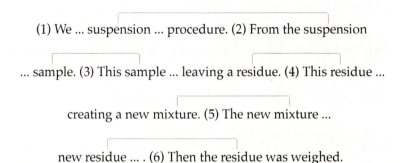

(1) We ... suspension ... procedure. (2) From the suspension

... sample. (3) This sample ... leaving a residue. (4) This residue ...

creating a new mixture. (5) The new mixture ...

new residue ... . (6) Then the residue was weighed.

Frankly, this revision verges on being overwritten; that is, it has more linkage than is probably necessary. The principal point is that you can usually achieve as much linkage as you desire. As the writer, you must judge how much linkage your readers need—how much can they read between the lines? If you expect readers to actually perform your procedure, then consider displaying the procedure step by step, as discussed in § 1.3.2.

Procedural paragraphs are used to document logical progressions, such as those that occur in experimental protocols, in computational algorithms, and in formal proofs. They are also used to document temporal progressions, such as those that pertain to sequences in biological processes and to the events that lead to mechanical failures and accidents. In addition, procedural paragraphs can be used together with metaphors to provide structure and imagery to abstractions. For example, the "quantum ladder" serves as a common metaphor for organizing descriptions of atomic energy levels. Here is a procedural paragraph describing three rungs on the ladder,

> This sequence is sometimes called the "quantum ladder"; it is defined by increases in energy. At the lowest rung of the ladder, matter is composed of individual atoms whose inner structures are inert and rigid; they move like billiard balls. At the next rung, atoms are decomposed into electrons and atomic nuclei, and these particles are viewed as individual units, inert and rigid. At the third rung, nuclei are decomposed into individual neutrons and protons; at this stage, the units of matter are protons, neutrons, and electrons. (paraphrased from Weisskopf [7])

In this example the linkage is not linear, but linearity is not required in procedural paragraphs; instead, linkage is achieved through the metaphor of the ladder—rung by rung. Metaphorical linkage is better than no linkage.

3.3 MECHANICS OF PARAGRAPHING

The human mind is a curious thing: it can confront and overcome all manner of difficulties, threats, and dangers—both real and imagined—yet it can be intimidated by a full page of type, a page unrelieved by any white space that might give an opportunity for momentary repose and reflection. When a page is crowded with black marks, the reader may be justifiably overwhelmed. Certainly such a presentation fails to accommodate the needs of the reader, for while the black marks on a page communicate something, the white space also communicates something—a fact understood by artists.

So give your readers a break—break your text into sensible paragraphs. By so doing we give readers psychological relief and we may help them digest the message. But when should we start a new paragraph? Here are some cues, though the following list is far from complete.

(1) When your central idea shifts, start a new paragraph. This is the standard guide: one idea, one paragraph. But often this guide is too simple: in some cases the development of a single idea may require several paragraphs or a whole thesis. Nevertheless, this simple guide provides a starting point for editing.

(2) When a paragraph gets too long, break it up. How long? As a maximum, one paragraph should be no longer than one page. This means paragraphing is influenced by the page size, the type size, and the spacing. Newspaper articles contain more paragraphs than books because in newspapers the type is small and the columns are narrow. Densely printed text should contain more paragraphs than sparsely printed text.

Related to this problem of length is one of balance. I'm not suggesting uniformity in length, but something more subtle having to do with offsetting short paragraphs with longer ones. This is partly aesthetics but also partly psychological—a continuous string of long paragraphs may intimidate some readers, a continuous string of short paragraphs may aggravate others.

Look through some well-written books just to see how paragraphs appear on the pages.

(3) When the structure of a paragraph changes, it may be appropriate to start a new paragraph. For example, the first five sentences of a paragraph may be in thematic form, then the next four may be linearly linked. Such a structural shift may signal the need for a new paragraph. But such a shift signals only a possibility, not a necessity. Before breaking that paragraph in two, you must consider the themes, how the last four sentences are linked to the first five, and what you want the emphasis to be. Those nine sentences may be better left as a single paragraph.

(4) When a paragraph has introduced too many different ideas too quickly, break it up. This situation often occurs because the writer has not given enough thought to the project, either in terms of becoming sufficiently familiar with the material or in terms of organizing the presentation or both.

(5) When descriptions become involved or explanations become complicated, help the reader by using more paragraphs. One prevalent complication involves nesting: you can't complete argument A until you've discussed point B, and you can't be convincing about B unless you prove deduction C. Your guiding strategy is divide and conquer; use paragraphs to communicate your divisions. In long explanations, you can help the reader by inserting an occasional paragraph that summarizes where you are in the development, what you have already accomplished, and what remains to be done.

3.4 Linking Large Structures

We have discussed linking elements into sentences and linking sentences into paragraphs, now we point out that paragraphs themselves should be linked into larger chunks, as sections or chapters. This usually poses few difficulties, but as the writer you should give attention to such linkage. Paragraph linkage is guided by our friend *old* → *new*; so when you start a new paragraph, start with an old idea—something the reader should recognize.

When a paragraph contributes to the body of a section, the linkage often connects to something in the previous paragraph. In these cases linkage can usually be established with small editorial adjustments applied to a few words, perhaps just one. However, more editorial attention must be given to the first paragraph in a chapter and to the first one in the whole work. In introductory paragraphs you should start with something that is known to both you and your reader, then you want to shift from that common knowledge to the theme of your presentation. Moreover you want to make that transition quickly but gracefully. Such transitions are not trivial pieces of writing; introductory paragraphs generally require careful planning and much editing. But at least you now know how to start.

Linkage contributes to coherence not only at the sentence and paragraph levels, but also at the section and chapter levels. This large-scale linkage is attained through such devices as introductions, summaries, and conclusions. These elements can be viewed as signposts that help guide the reader through a document: they should help the reader keep focussed on the objectives, help the reader connect sections and chapters into a logical whole, and help the reader locate the writing within a larger context. To be effective, large linking elements should communicate a document's organizational structure, and therefore a document must be designed to have a structure that can be communicated. In a loose rambling discourse the emphasis is likely to be so diffuse and the coherence so muddled that the reader will be confused rather than enlightened, and the writer's effort will be wasted.

Introductions and summaries often pose special writing problems because they require a shift in thinking. Many technical people function best when concentrating on technical details, but to write effective large-scale linkage we must overlook details in favor of a more comprehensive view. Technical writers often devise strategies that help them achieve sound large-scale linkage. For example, some writers compose the introduction and summary first, and then they use those drafts to guide the drafting of intermediate sections. Others compose the introductions and summaries last, using the intermediate sections to guide the drafting of the linkage. No matter what drafting strategy you use, you should give introductions, summaries, and conclusions final editorial attention after all other parts have been edited. One test for effective linking elements is this: try to judge what would be gained if a reader skipped the body of each chapter and read only the introductions, summaries, and conclusions. Those sections should reveal the logical path taken through the material and they should contain your principal points of emphasis; the path and the points along the path should be stated explicitly and directly.

3.5 SUMMARY

In this chapter we have presented some simple ways that can be used to organize sentences into coherent paragraphs. To achieve coherence, sentences must be clearly linked, and effective linkage is realized through repetition and proximity: repetition dominates sentence-to-theme linkage, while proximity dominates sentence-to-sentence linkage.

But how do we decide what form a paragraph should take? The answer depends on what the paragraph is intended to accomplish and what we want to emphasize. For example, if the paragraph is to develop a logical argument, then the linear form is appropriate; however, if the paragraph is to summarize the beneficial aspects of a thing, then the thematic form may be preferred. The role of a particular paragraph often remains unclear during drafting; frequently our intentions clarify only during editing. So it is usually during editing that we determine what kind of structure a paragraph should have, and then we rewrite the linkage accordingly.

But further, most paragraphs do not conform to any one of the simple structures presented in this chapter; instead, many are compounds of two or more simple structures. Such compounds can certainly be legitimate and effective, so long as their linkages are clear. If you are familiar with the simple structures discussed here, then you will be able to recognize other simple structures and recognize when simple structures are being combined into more complex forms. When you can detect patterns, editing is less burdensome.

EXERCISES

3.1 Consider the following paragraph:

> Our strategy is called iterative design. In an iterative design we teach ourselves how to accomplish a complex task by first mastering a simplified model and then systematically adding complications. The intent is to solve a formidable problem, in the end, by a straight-forward combination of less complicated elements.

(a) Revise this into the form of a thematic paragraph.
(b) Revise it again into a linear paragraph.

3.2 Consider this paragraph:

> Texts and other technical documents are not like novels, and they should not be read in the same linear way that novels are read. Not only does technical writing employ jargon that must be deciphered, but it also uses equations, graphs, and tables to communicate a large amount of information in a clear, economical fashion. Simply reading and rereading a chapter of a text is not an effective way to learn.

(a) Revise this into one form of sentence-to-theme linkage.
(b) Revise it again into one form of sentence-to-sentence linkage.

3.3 Consider this paragraph:

> At this point we have models for much of the pure-fluid phase diagram, but thus far, every model applies to only one phase—either gas or liquid. We would prefer to have a single model that could be used for both gases and liquids. Such models would have to be more complex than any of the previous ones, but we would prefer that they not be too complex; we would like the algebraic forms to contain a small number of terms with few adjustable parameters. Thus, we face the usual conflict between physical realism and mathematical complexity.

(a) Revise this into a radial paragraph.

(b) Revise it again into a thematic paragraph.

(c) Revise yet again into a linear paragraph.

3.4 Consider this paragraph:

> Most inefficiencies in waterwheels occur as frictional losses in the gearing that converts rotary motion of the wheel into useful work. Ancient wheels typically managed to convert 10-20% of the available energy into useful work. By the turn of the 19th century, efficiencies had reached 60%. Nevertheless, even ancient wheels were more powerful and reliable than animal labor. One person can provide only about 100 watts of sustained power, and cattle can deliver about 300 watts per head. But an ancient Roman waterwheel could deliver 2000 watts.

(a) Revise this into a radial paragraph.

(b) Revise it again into a thematic paragraph.

(c) Revise yet again into a linear paragraph.

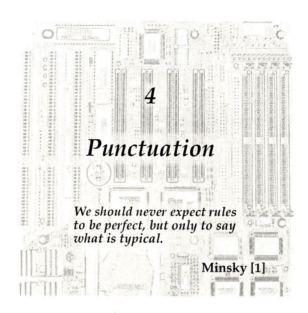

4

Punctuation

We should never expect rules to be perfect, but only to say what is typical.

Minsky [1]

Although style is not determined solely by grammatical correctness, style is certainly influenced by grammatical usage. For example, faulty punctuation implies a careless writer—one who fails to anticipate the needs of the reader. In this chapter we briefly review those rules of punctuation that are most often violated in technical writing. For more thorough explanations of punctuation, consult a standard grammar such as Harbrace [2], or a style manual for your discipline, such as that published by the American Chemical Society [3].

All punctuation is intended to forestall ambiguities, but in addition, punctuation constitutes a small but important element of style. The controlled use of commas, semicolons, and the occasional dash suggests a kind of writing rather different from that which relies heavily on commas and little else. The marks of punctuation are tools in the writer's toolbox, and competent craftsmen know how to use all their tools.

4.1 COMMA

In an earlier age commas were used liberally, often to signal points for breathing when the text was read aloud. Modern writing tends toward a sparse usage of commas—often breathtakingly sparse—for without the guidance provided by well-placed commas, reading can become tentative and halting. Commas prevent ambiguities by showing how phrases link; as an example, consider this sentence:

> In every case we have checked the data and (E4.1)
> the results are the same.

This sentence seems innocent enough, but in fact it can be interpreted in at least two ways. It might mean this,

> In every case, we have checked the data, and (E4.2)
> the results are the same.

or it might mean this,

> In every case we have checked, the data and (E4.3)
> the results are the same.

We use commas to help communicate the intended meaning; so during editing, we must be sensitive to ambiguous structures, such as (E4.1), and punctuate appropriately.

But in addition to removing ambiguities, commas can also indicate subtle aspects of sentence structure; they can show how we intend words to be grouped into phrases. This grouping of words influences meaning, of course, but it can also suggest a cadence or rhythm that seems central to a pleasing style. This secondary usage of the comma is somewhat analogous to the long slurs used to indicate phrasing in musical scores. I doubt whether this kind of subtlety can be taught, but I think it can be learned by reading the works of gifted writers.

4.1.1 USE A COMMA TO JOIN TWO MAIN CLAUSES

When a sentence is formed from two main clauses joined by a conjunction, place a comma before the conjunction.

> The last term in the series is negligible,   (E4.4)
> and it can be ignored.

However, if the conjunction does not join complete clauses, the comma must be omitted,

> The last term in the series is negligible   (E4.5)
> and can be ignored.

4.1.2 USE COMMAS TO INDICATE A NONRESTRICTIVE PHRASE

If a subordinate phrase adds information without affecting meaning, then it is nonrestrictive. The test is whether the phrase can be omitted: if leaving out the phrase does not change the meaning of the sentence, then the phrase is nonrestrictive and it should be set off with commas. Otherwise, the phrase is restrictive, and commas should not be used.

Restrictive and nonrestrictive phrases modify a noun that identifies a set or class. Nonrestrictive phrases apply to all members of the set, for example,

> We realize that these results, shown   (E4.6)
> in Figure 10, are wrong.

In this example "these results" identifies the set of results under discussion, and all members of the set appear in Figure 10. The nonrestrictive phrase could be safely omitted,

> We realize that these results are wrong.   (R4.6)

But a restrictive phrase applies only to certain members of the set, for example,

> We realize that the results shown in Figure 10 (E4.7)
> are wrong.

Here "shown in Figure 10" limits the wrong results to a subset of all results; that is, presumably there are other results that are not in Figure 10 and that are not wrong. The absence of commas indicates that the phrase is restrictive.

4.1.3 USE A COMMA AFTER MOST INTRODUCTORY PHRASES

A comma generally helps signal the transition from an introductory phrase to the main clause,

> To test this hypothesis, we performed more (E4.8)
> experiments at high temperatures.

When the introductory phrase is long, a comma is always required, not only to mark the transition but also to give the reader a brief respite.

> If the blood samples had not been contaminated (E4.9)
> so thoroughly, the damaged cells would not
> have been discovered.

But when the introductory phrase is short, we may omit the comma, so long as the meaning is unaffected,

> To test this we did more experiments. (E4.10)

Whether we actually omit the comma depends on what we judge will satisfy the needs of the reader. If you feel the reader may have to read a sentence more than once to decode the structure, then insert the comma; if you have any doubt, insert the comma.

Modern usage tends to omit the comma when a sentence starts with a single linking word, such as *however,* or with a standard linking phrase, such as *for example.* But the comma must be inserted if its omission could produce an ambiguity. Consider this sentence:

> However improved trial-and-error algorithms   (E4.11)
> do not always converge.

Here the lack of a comma makes the sentence unclear; it could mean

> However, improved trial-and-error algorithms   (E4.12)
> do not always converge.

In this interpretation, the introductory *however* means *nevertheless.* But (E4.11) might also mean

> However improved, trial-and-error algorithms   (E4.13)
> do not always converge.

Now the *however* means *no matter how,* so that (E4.13) carries a meaning considerably different from that in (E4.12).

Placing commas after introductory words and phrases requires sensitive editing—a blind consistency fails to serve. Using a comma after every introductory phrase can create a disjointed structure that may antagonize modern readers. Omitting the comma from every introductory phrase will eventually produce ambiguities that frustrate all readers. This is an issue that must be guided by a flexible attitude, informed judgement, and good taste.

4.1.4 USE COMMAS TO SEPARATE ITEMS IN A SERIES

Three or more items in a series must be separated by commas,

> The tank contained a mixture of water,   (E4.14)
> champagne, orange juice, and pineapple juice.

The issue is whether a comma should be placed before the conjunction. Make it a habit to do so, else some sequences may be ambiguous; for example,

> The tank was fed by streams of water,   (E4.15)
> champagne, orange juice and pineapple juice.

How many streams fed the tank, three or four? The reader cannot judge; there might have been only three, with the third carrying a mixture of orange and pineapple juices.

More troublesome are sequences of adjectives. If two or more adjectives, all of equal importance, modify the same noun, then use commas to separate the adjectives.

> This was a difficult, exasperating, laborious   (E4.16)
> experiment.

The test for importance is whether the adjectives can be reordered without changing the meaning. If the positions can be safely permuted, then the adjectives are of equal weight, and commas are used. Thus the meaning of (E4.16) is unchanged if we write

> This was a laborious, difficult, exasperating   (R4.16)
> experiment.

However, if some words in the sequence are serving as adverbs to modify some of the adjectives, then the words are not all of equal importance, their order cannot be freely permuted, and commas may be omitted. For example,

> This was a difficult high frequency experiment. (E4.17)

4.2 SEMICOLON

To join two complete clauses we often use a conjunction; however, in many sentences we could also use a semicolon. For example, the *and* in (E4.4) could be replaced with a semicolon,

> The last term in the series is negligible; it can (E4.18)
> be ignored.

Of course, the conjunction could also be replaced by a period:

> The last term in the series is negligible. It can (E4.19)
> be ignored.

So when should we use a semicolon rather than a conjunction or a period? One consideration is length: if both clauses are short, as in (E4.18), then a conjunction is usually preferred. But if both clauses are very long, then the better choice is probably to use a period to break the sentence in two. The semicolon is often the best choice when the clauses are of intermediate length and when the second clause is closely related to the first. For example, the semicolon is appropriate when the second clause amplifies, illustrates, or is a consequence of the first.

In technical writing the semicolon seems to be most often used in this grammatical structure:

> First main clause; linking phrase, second main (E4.20)
> clause.

When the second clause is a consequence of or a deduction from the first, the linking phrase may be *hence, therefore, thus,* or *consequently.* If the second phrase illustrates the first, the linking phrase might be *for example.* If it provides an exception to the first, the link could be *instead* or *in contrast,* and if it amplifies or adds to the first, then *further, furthermore, moreover,* or *in addition* could provide the linkage.

The semicolon may also be used to separate items in a series, when the items themselves contain commas. Thus the semicolon may be used as a super-comma; for example,

> The tank was fed by three streams: one contained (E4.21)
> orange juice, water, and champagne; the second
> orange juice, pineapple juice, and ice; the third
> only ginger ale and champagne.

When used in this way, the semicolon separates rather than joins, and then the semicolon need not be preceded by a complete clause.

Looking beyond individual sentences, we find that the semicolon may help preserve the linkage of sentences in a paragraph. As an example, consider this paragraph (a paraphrase from Weisskopf [4]),

> This sequence is sometimes called the "quantum ladder"; it is defined by increases in energy. At the lowest rung of the ladder, matter is composed of individual atoms whose inner structures are inert and rigid; they move like billiard balls. At the next rung, atoms are decomposed into electrons and atomic nuclei, and these particles are viewed as individual units, inert and rigid. At the third rung, nuclei are decomposed into individual neutrons and protons; at this stage, the units of matter are protons, neutrons, and electrons.

We used this paragraph in § 3.2.3 to show how a procedural paragraph can be employed to discuss an abstract concept in concrete terms. In this paragraph the sentences are linked through the metaphor of the ladder: the second, third, and fourth sentences each start by referring to a rung on the ladder.

Note the three semicolons. In each usage, a semicolon seems to be the best choice, as opposed to either a conjunction or a period. A conjunction would not be as strong; for example, *and* would seem to be particularly weak. Alternatively, replacing the semicolon with a period proves disruptive:

> At the third rung, nuclei are decomposed   (E4.22)
> into individual neutrons and protons. At
> this stage, the units of matter are protons,
> neutrons, and electrons.

Not only does the period unnecessarily separate closely connected clauses, but the period also interferes with the established linkage. While previous sentences link to rungs on the ladder, the new last sentence in (E4.22) does not; instead, it amplifies ideas introduced in the previous sentence, and therefore it reads as a superfluous afterthought. So when editing paragraphs, remember that the semicolon can serve as a valuable device for maintaining appropriate linkage among sentences.

4.3 COLON

When a phrase or clause B illustrates, amplifies, or exemplifies another clause A, then a colon can be used to denote the relation between the two, A:B. The colon serves to draw the reader's attention to B by visually separating B from A. The grammatical object A, which precedes the colon, must *always* be a complete clause. However, no constraints apply to B: it may be a list, or an equation, or another complete clause, like the one you've just read. Therefore, never insert a colon between a verb and its object, between a verb and a predicate noun or predicate adjective, or between a preposition and its object. Never write

> The tank contained: water, orange juice, **(wrong)** (E4.23) and champagne.

If you want a colon, precede it with a complete thought:

> The tank contained the following: water, (E4.24) orange juice, and champagne.

But when would we write (E4.24) rather than the following more sedate form?

> The tank contained water, orange juice, and (E4.25) champagne.

In most situations we would use (E4.25) rather than (E4.24). The colon should be used only when we wanted to draw extra attention to the contents of the tank. Note that in (E4.25) the water, juice, and champagne already occupy a point of emphasis—the end of the sentence. The colon serves to heighten the emphasis by pushing the end of the sentence further from its body. Thus the colon should be used sparingly, else the reader's sensitivity becomes dulled by overemphasis.

When A and B are both complete clauses, the colon replaces any linking conjunction. But when should two complete clauses be separated by a colon, rather than be joined by a semicolon? The colon should be used when the first clause serves to introduce or prepare for the second; the first clause A only serves to link B to some earlier idea. In such sentences the important idea resides in the second clause B, and it receives double emphasis by being at the end of the sentence and by being preceded by the colon.

In contrast, we use a semicolon when the clauses A and B are of roughly equal importance; A is not merely introducing B, though B may be a consequence of A. When we use a semicolon to join two clauses, we are implying that the two are closely related; we are also implying that the relation might be overlooked if the two were separated by a conjunction or a period. But when we insert a colon between two clauses, we are separating the two, not joining them, so as to achieve extra emphasis.

4.4 DASH

To signal an abrupt change of thought, use a dash. For example, use dashes to separate a parenthetical phrase from the rest of a sentence. This usage is of particular value when the parenthetical phrase itself contains commas—colons, semicolons, and periods rarely occur in multiples—thereby clearly delineating the parenthetical phrase.

The dash may also be used in place of a colon (A—B) when the transition from the introductory clause A to the subsequent phrase B is abrupt and when we want heavy emphasis on B. In this use the dash adds even more emphasis than the colon because it pushes the end of the sentence B farther from the main clause A. This usage is particularly effective when B is a short phrase—not a main clause.

The dash appears to be neglected by many writers, which seems a pity for it is a worthy object and fun to use. Of course, overuse would be detrimental, but, used infrequently and with care, the dash can add a flourish to your writing.

4.5 HYPHEN

The principal use of the hyphen is to join two or more words to form a single unit, when that unit is to modify a single noun. As writers we must exercise our own discretion as to when hyphenation is needed, although we should also adhere to the conventions of our disciplines. For example, the three-word unit *trial and error* is hyphenated when used as an adjective,

> Newton's method is a trial-and-error scheme (E4.26)
> for obtaining the roots of nonlinear equations.

But when it is used as a noun, the hyphens should be omitted:

> The equation was solved by trial and error. (E4.27)

More importantly, hyphens should be used when sequences of adjectives are ambiguous. Thus,

> To calculate the maximum profit margin, we (E4.28)
> added an extra cost term to the objective function.

Here, the phrase "extra cost term" is unclear: was the thing an "extra-cost term" or an "extra cost-term"? A hyphen removes the ambiguity.

4.6 SUMMARY

We have briefly reviewed a system of sentence punctuation based on five points: the period, dash, colon, semicolon, and comma. The period, dash, and colon are used in only a few well-defined ways, and so their deployment should cause little difficulty. Somewhat more troublesome is the semicolon, which stands midway between a comma and a period: the semicolon connects two complete clauses by imposing a break that is stronger than one provided by a comma but weaker than one marked by a period.

Because it is the most versatile mark of punctuation, the comma is open to the most abuse. The abuse may take the form of misuse or overuse or both. Misuse can be cured by knowing the rules of grammar and following those rules when they clearly apply. But overuse of commas is less easily resolved; often, overuse is symptomatic of weak sentence structure, and the problem can be cured by crafting each sentence so that the structure itself avoids ambiguities. Then the comma is needed only occasionally, not to impose a structure, but merely to reinforce it.

EXERCISES

4.1 Punctuate the following sentences.

(a) For example the fuel line has sprung a leak downstream of the fuel pump so gasoline is being pumped onto the hot engine block and the gas ignites.

(b) In a balanced chemical reaction absolute values of stoichiometric coefficients are not fixed however ratios of any two coefficients are fixed by the balance.

(c) We restrict our attention to pure substances we are also interested in mixtures but the theoretical tools for analyzing mixtures have not yet been developed.

(d) Adiabatic processes occur often in practice and when they do Equation (15.7) allows us to compute work effects exactly without having to account explicitly for irreversibilities.

(e) Use of a model invokes an approximation and it is an act of engineering judgment to decide whether any errors associated with a model can be tolerated within the context of the particular problem situation.

(f) Heat effects are divided into two types sensible effects in which the system temperature changes and latent effects in which the system temperature remains constant.

(g) When solving a problem you should understand not only what you are doing but also why you are doing it.

(h) Although energy is not an object we often talk as if it were for example we may talk about the amount of energy stored in common fuels.

(i) Sometimes this approximation is exactly right such as when it is used for ideal gas mixtures and sometimes it is nearly right such as for ethanol water mixtures.

(j) Each such response is the same property which is given a special name the chemical potential.

(k) In this section we consider first material balances for binary mixtures and second balances for multicomponent mixtures.

(l) In an analysis we know the inputs to a process and we must compute the outputs while in a design we know the outputs and we must compute the inputs.

(m) In such situations engineering judgment must be employed to decide whether a particular pressure is low moderate or high.

(n) In some situations more than one chemical reaction may compete for the same reactants and a catalyst might be used to accelerate the desired reaction effectively selecting one reaction over the others.

4.2 Punctuate this paragraph.

Thermal interaction by radiation refers to electromagnetic waves such as those from the sun and those in a microwave oven the typical microwave oven is tuned to frequencies that correspond to the rotational motion of water molecules when you microwave a candy bar you are stimulating water molecules to rotate faster increasing their thermal energy this thermal energy is then transferred by conduction from the water to other molecules in the candy.

4.3 The following is the first draft of a letter reporting the results obtained by a design team. List all errors that you can find in word usage, sentence structure, linkage, paragraphing, and punctuation. You should also list any errors of fact and of form that you find.

29 February 2002

Dr. William P. Magillicutty, Senior Engineer
Chrysalis Engineering, LLC.
26 Tidewater Avenue
High Time, VA

Re: The Flowing Experiment

Dear Billy,

Upon receiving the list of objectives for the group to tackle, an in-depth experiment to determine the roughness of various pipes with several materials and diameters was began. The data that was obtained for the roughness was compared with literature for clean pipes to find out how much corrosion there was. Along with this, the design of a flow metering system has been included utilizing a two-way double flow meter with multiple sampling ports.

The experiment was accomplished using several pipes: brass and galvanized as well as PVC, respectively. Flowrates and pressuredrops were obtained across each pipes. The flowrates were obtained by letting the water run into a bucket sitting on a scales. The initial and final buckets were recorded for some times. The pressures were obtained from an oil and a mercury manometers.

Once the data was found, calculations of friction factors and Reynold's numbers were completed. This data was used to compare with theoretical results from the literature. The comparison was pretty good, except for one pipe. Finally, the various flow rates encountered were used to design a flow meter that will deliver the actual flow rates of the pipes used. The design is reported in Appendix A.

The results from the data are given in the Figures; mainly we learned that the flow meter needs to be positioned in the center of the pipe diameter. The results would have been better if a flowmeter was already on the pipes so we wouldn't have to use the bucket and scales. This took quality time away from the experiment.

Very truly yours,

Chuck Wood

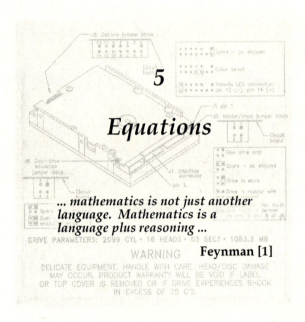

5

Equations

... mathematics is not just another language. Mathematics is a language plus reasoning ...

Feynman [1]

While the basic rules of grammar and the elements of style are common to most forms of writing, technical writing is unique in its use of equations. Nevertheless, books on technical writing often ignore the problems writers face in presenting equations and the problems readers face in decoding them. Creating and decoding equations both require an ability to interpret physical objects in terms of the abstractions of language and mathematics, and achieving such interpretations is far from trivial. If equations are to be interpreted easily and correctly, then the abstract symbols in equations must be explicitly connected to mathematical and physical realities. We emphasize that connections should be explicit; difficulties in decoding equations usually occur because writers and readers tacitly attach incomplete or erroneous meanings to symbols or terms or even entire equations.

An equation is a more substantial device than a mere formula. A *formula* provides an algorithm for transforming numbers into other numbers; an example is the quadratic formula, which gives the roots to quadratic equations. But an *equation* asserts a relation among ideas; an example is Einstein's equation $E = mc^2$, which establishes an equivalence between mass and energy. It is true that many equations can also serve as formulae for calculations, but this fact contributes little to their role as aids for organizing thought.

Not only do equations relate ideas, but they do so in economical ways: with just a few symbols, equations can convey complex and sophisticated relations. But their power to communicate carries with it the power to confuse, and so equations must be subjected to the same care in preparation and editorial attention as other aspects of technical writing.

In this chapter we discuss the value of a good notation (§ 5.1), and we summarize the conventions used to display equations properly (§ 5.2). Then we argue that readers are helped when equations are presented in economical forms (§ 5.3) and when equations are supplemented with alternative interpretations (§ 5.4). Such interpretations may be physical (§ 5.4.1), mathematical (§ 5.4.2), or graphical (§ 5.4.3).

5.1 NOTATION

We use equations not only to achieve economy of expression, but also to take advantage of the rules of mathematical reasoning. An equation represents a closed universe in which each symbol has a clearly articulated and unambiguous meaning; moreover, the symbols can only be manipulated in ways that preserve logical and mathematical consistency. Thus if two people can agree on the validity of a particular equation, then they must also agree on any deduction obtained by performing allowed operations on the initial equation. This kind of reasoning, which we take for granted, is hardly known in other disciplines, such as politics or law, where two people can start from the same premise and reach contradictory conclusions.

Constructing an equation is an act of translation from ordinary language to the language of mathematics. But writers should keep in mind that their readers face the inverse problem: readers must translate the mathematical language of equations back into ordinary language. Translations are hindered by a notation that is cumbersome and obscure, so don't underestimate the power of a well-chosen notation to facilitate translations [2].

To the extent possible, use symbols whose meanings have become conventional in your discipline—symbols that are familiar to your readers. For example, in algebra a, b, and c are conventionally used as parameters; x, y, and z are used to represent unknowns; i, j, and k are usually used as dummy subscripts and indices for sums and products. Ignoring convention without good reason will almost certainly promote confusion among readers. Inversely, don't abuse conventional symbols by using them in unconventional ways; thus, reserve e and π for their standard meanings.

Conventions also apply to fonts and font-styles. Thus, plain-face type is used for scalars, bold-face for vectors, and bold upper-case sans serif for matrices and tensors. In geometry, upper-case Roman is used to label vertices of plane figures, lower-case Roman for sides, and lower-case Greek for angles. In displays of computational algorithms in pseudocode, the convention is to use a monospaced font rather than a proportionally spaced one.

A good notation is easily remembered, and one simple aid to the memory is to use initials for symbols. For example, in thermodynamics we conventionally use T for temperature, P for pressure, and V for volume. In classical mechanics the expression

$$\Phi = \mu\alpha \qquad (5.1)$$

carries little meaning; but in the form

$$F = ma \qquad (5.2)$$

we immediately recognize Newton's second law.

Don't confuse readers by using the same symbol for two different things. On the other hand, readers may be helped by showing them that two different symbols can be applied to the same thing. In Newton's second law, the acceleration a can be expressed as the time rate of change of velocity v, so (5.2) could also be written as

$$F = m\frac{dv}{dt} \qquad (5.3)$$

Using more than one symbol for the same thing can help some readers connect new ideas to familiar ones; the value in helping readers make connections is discussed further in § 5.4.

Another device for simplifying notation is to use similar symbols for similar things. For example, if N represents the number of moles in a sample, then $\mathcal{N}$ could represent the number of molecules in the same sample. This strategy can be extended by keeping the same symbol and adding subscripts and superscripts to distinguish similar things. For example, in theories of solutions V is typically used to denote the volume of a mixture; then other kinds of volume-like quantities are defined and represented by some embellished V:

V_r = the residual volume of the mixture   (5.4a)

V^E = the excess volume of the mixture   (5.4b)

Superscripts and subscripts are also used to label the members of a set. Thus the interior angles of a plane irregular hexagon could be effectively represented by $\{\alpha\} = \alpha_1, \alpha_2, \alpha_3, \alpha_4, \alpha_5, \alpha_6$.

Here are some cautions in creating superscripts and subscripts: (a) Don't use a superscript or subscript if it is not needed to convey distinctions—if, for example, your set contains only a single member. (b) Avoid overloading a single symbol with multiple superscripts and subscripts, else the communication is obscured rather than facilitated. (c) Likewise, don't venture beyond second-level subscripts. For example, in V_{H_2O} the second level 2 is tolerable, but additional sublevels should be avoided. (d) Keep superscripts and subscripts short; as a rule of thumb, use no more than three letters. Thus V_r is better than $V_{residual}$.

5.2 Mechanics of Presentation

To emphasize an equation we set it on a line by itself and use white space to separate it from surrounding text; this is called a *display*. Only short simple equations should be presented within the text, and even those should normally be displayed. In this section we summarize the principal conventions for displaying equations [3].

5.2.1 Punctuation

Publishing houses are divided as to whether equations should be punctuated; in my view they should not. In mathematical expressions commas and periods can confuse and aggravate the reader. Recall that the purpose of punctuation is to prevent ambiguities, usually by inserting a pause that signals a logical break in the message. By displaying an equation, we have already inserted a visual break, and that break is not enhanced by including a comma or period. To gain meaning from equations, they cannot be read in the same way we read text; if an equation is new to the reader or if it involves any complexity at all, then it must claim the reader's attention for some considerable time. Punctuation in equations is superfluous.

But when we omit punctuation from equations, we must carefully edit the surrounding phrases so that their structures are clear and their meanings unambiguous. This is rarely difficult to achieve. Usually the equation is the important part of its sentence, and therefore the equation should appear near the end. To signal that an equation occurs at the very end of a sentence, we start the next line of text with an upper-case letter.

Of course, we must correctly punctuate those phrases that appear immediately before and after a displayed equation. In particular, do *not* precede an equation with a comma (§ 4.1) or a colon (§ 4.3) unless such marks are grammatically correct. For example,

In a right triangle the hypotenuse c is related
to the sides a and b by: (**wrong**)

$$c^2 = a^2 + b^2 \qquad (5.5a)$$

In a right triangle the hypotenuse c is related
to the sides a and b by   (**right**)

$$c^2 = a^2 + b^2 \qquad (5.5b)$$

In a right triangle the hypotenuse c is related to
the sides a and b by the Pythagorean theorem: (**right**)

$$c^2 = a^2 + b^2 \qquad (5.5c)$$

5.2.2 EQUATION NUMBERS

Most authorities suggest that equation numbers be placed only on those equations that the author explicitly cites in the text; in this view, equation numbers aid the writer. This seems misguided. Equation numbers, like everything else on the page, should aid the reader, and since the reader may want to refer to *any* displayed equation, they should *all* be numbered. This is especially important in textbooks, teaching literature, and tutorial documents, for instructors and students may need to refer to equations not explicitly cited by the author. Equation numbers are not part of the text, they are part of the documentary structure—like page numbers. All pages are numbered; likewise, all equations should be numbered.

5.2.3 SIGNS FOR OPERATORS AND FOR AGGREGATION

For the minus sign use the em-dash (–), not the smaller en-dash (-), which is difficult to see. When a sign is needed to indicate multiplication, use the sans serif character ($\times$)—if it is available—rather than the serif letter (x) or the raised dot (•). When expressions are nested, the signs of aggregation should be ordered like this: $\{\,[\,(\,\{\,[\,(\;\;)\,]\,\}\,)\,]\,\}$.

5.2.4 ELISIONS

When terms are omitted from a series or sequence, the ellipsis should be preceded and followed by a comma or an operator, as appropriate.

Write $a_1 + a_2 + \ldots + a_n$ not $a_1 + a_2 \ldots a_n$.

Write $a_1, a_2, \ldots, a_n$ not $a_1, a_2, \ldots a_n$.

If the sequence forms a product, then no comma or operator should be used; for example, a product could be correctly written as $a_1 a_2 \ldots a_n$.

5.2.5 FRACTIONS

When writing fractions we must choose either the horizontal *bar* (—) or the *solidus* (/). Fractions presented within the text should always use the solidus; for example, $n(n + 1)/2$. But in displayed equations a fraction should usually be written with the bar:

$$\sum_{i=1}^{n} i = \frac{n(n+1)}{2} = \frac{n}{2}(n+1) \tag{5.6}$$

Use the solidus for fractions that appear in the numerator or denominator of displayed fractions:

$$x = \frac{a}{c/d - 1} + \frac{b/4 + b^2}{c} \tag{5.7}$$

Likewise, use the solidus for fractions that appear in exponents, integration limits, and indices on sums and products:

$$z = (a + b)^{(x+y)/2} \tag{5.8}$$

$$z = \int_{a/b}^{b/a} f(x)\, dx \tag{5.9}$$

$$z = \sum_{i=a/b}^{n} x_i \tag{5.10}$$

Develop the habit of preceding all decimal fractions with a zero, 0.25 not .25; this applies to decimals appearing in text, tables, and figures. Avoid using both decimal and numerical fractions in the same sentence; decimal fractions are preferred over numerical ones,

The sample had a mass of 1/3 kg and an area of 0.5 m². **(wrong)**

The sample had a mass of 0.33 kg and an area of 0.5 m². **(right)**

5.2.6 EXPONENTIALS

When the exponential operator *e* and its argument appear in the text, always use the *exp*-form. In displayed equations, use the *exp*-form if the exponent contains an integral sign, a summation sign, a radical, or is otherwise complicated,

$$z = \exp\left[\int_0^\infty f(x)\,dx\right] \tag{5.11}$$

5.2.7 SCIENTIFIC NOTATION

In all text, tables, and figures use correct scientific notation; do not use computer jargon.

6.023E23 and 6.023*10**23 **(wrong)**

$6.023(10^{23})$ and 6.023×10^{23} **(right)**

5.2.8 SPACING

Leave space around operators, equal signs, and inequalities, but omit the space in superscripts and subscripts:

$$N_A = 6.023 \times 10^{23} \tag{5.12}$$

Do not insert space after numerical coefficients.

$$w = 2a + 3(b - c)^{(x + y)} \tag{5.13}$$

In such operators as *sin, cos, ln,* and *exp,* use a space to separate the operator from its argument, but omit the space if the argument is enclosed in some sign of aggregation:

$$\sin(x + y) = \sin x \cos y + \cos x \sin y \tag{5.14}$$

$$\ln(\sin x) = \ln x - \frac{x^2}{6} - \frac{x^4}{180} - \dots \tag{5.15}$$

Insert a single space before and after the combined pair of differential operator plus its argument and the delta operator plus its argument.

$$A = \int f(x, y)\, dx\, dy \tag{5.16}$$

$$m\, \Delta v^2 = m(v_2^2 - v_1^2) \tag{5.17}$$

5.2.9 BREAKING LONG EQUATIONS

When an equation must occupy more than one line, try to make each break before a sum or difference operator, but in any case start each successive line with an operator. The operator should be aligned to the right of the equal sign

$$d(NF) = N\left(\frac{\partial F}{\partial T}\right)_{PN} + N\sum_i \left[\frac{\partial(NF)}{\partial N_i}\right]_{TPN_{j \neq i}} dx_i \tag{5.18}$$

$$+ N\left(\frac{\partial F}{\partial P}\right)_{TN} + \sum_i \left[\frac{\partial(NF)}{\partial N_i}\right]_{TPN_{j \neq i}} x_i\, dN$$

$$\int x^m (a+bx)^n \, dx = \frac{x^{(m+1)}(a+bx)^n}{m+n+1} + \frac{an}{m+n+1} \qquad (5.19)$$

$$\times \int x^m (a+bx)^{(n-1)} \, dx$$

Alternatively, consider keeping the equation to a single line by using a symbol for each term; for example, (5.19) could be presented in this form:

$$\int x^m (a+bx)^n \, dx = A + B \qquad (5.20)$$

where

$$A = \frac{x^{(m+1)}(a+bx)^n}{m+n+1} \qquad (5.21)$$

and

$$B = \frac{an}{m+n+1} \int x^m (a+bx)^{(n-1)} \, dx \qquad (5.22)$$

Although (5.20)-(5.22) take more space than (5.19), they are usually easier to type and easier for readers to assimilate.

5.2.10 IDENTIFYING VARIABLES

Readers are helped in their efforts to understand displayed equations when variables are identified immediately after an equation. This is worth doing even when you give a list of symbols elsewhere in the document. For example,

For an arbitrary plane triangle, the law of cosines states

$$c^2 = a^2 + b^2 - 2ab \cos C \qquad (5.23)$$

where a, b, and c are the lengths of the three sides and C is the angle opposite side c.

The identification is generally more graceful when you use verbs rather than equal signs ("C is the ... " , rather than "C = the ... "). Typically a symbol needs to be identified only when it first appears, though you may want to remind readers of an identification if several pages have intervened since a symbol was used.

5.3 ECONOMICAL DISPLAY

The rules of display in § 5.2 are intended to help the reader get the message; in particular, displayed equations are intended to help readers see relations. And readers more readily grasp relations when the equations are structurally simple, unencumbered by distracting embellishments. Even when an equation is intended to be used as a formula for computing, the chances for computational errors are reduced by presenting the formula in a way that emphasizes relations among variables. For example, here is a formula for determining how temperature T affects the hydroxide ion concentration C_{OH} in a certain solution:

$$C_{OH} = 10^{[7.0 - 14.92 + 4.03e - 2T(C) - 1.4e - 4T(C)^2]} \qquad (5.24)$$

This example has multiple problems: it does not employ proper scientific notation, it fails to make clear whether the final T should be squared, and it confuses the unit of temperature, (°C) in the exponent, with the concentration, C on the left. Taken together, these faults obscure the relation between concentration C and temperature T; in fact, the logarithm of C is quadratic in T. To clarify that relation, we simplify (5.24) to

$$\log C = a_0 + a_1 T + a_2 T^2 \qquad (5.25)$$

where $a_0 = -7.92$, $a_1 = 0.0403$, $a_2 = -1.41(10^{-4})$, and T is in °C. To generalize the lessons from (5.24), never include units in equations, and rarely include values for parameters; instead, cite units and values in the sentence(s) following the display.

Relations are often obscured and equations made uneconomical by redundancies: the repeated use of the same group of terms. Such redundancies usually add clutter, making equations appear unnecessarily complicated. For example,

$$L = \sum_i \left\{ y_i \ln \left[\frac{\exp(\beta_0 + \sigma_i \beta_1)}{1 + \exp(\beta_0 + \sigma_i \beta_1)} \right] \right. \qquad (5.26)$$

$$\left. + \ (1 - y_i) \ln \left[1 - \frac{\exp(\beta_0 + \sigma_i \beta_1)}{1 + \exp(\beta_0 + \sigma_i \beta_1)} \right] \right\}$$

But if we let

$$B_i = \frac{\exp(\beta_0 + \sigma_i \beta_1)}{1 + \exp(\beta_0 + \sigma_i \beta_1)} \qquad (5.27)$$

then the structure of (5.26) is more clearly revealed:

$$L = \sum_i [y_i \ln B_i + (1 - y_i) \ln(1 - B_i)] \qquad (5.28)$$

Although (5.26) requires three levels of nesting { [( )] }, the revision (5.28) needs only two [( )].

Removing redundancies not only simplifies, but occasionally it may also suggest that certain combinations of variables are more important than individual variables. Consider this example,

$$C = \frac{4ae^{\frac{uL}{2D}}}{(1+a)^2 e^{\frac{uL}{2D}} - (1-a)^2 e^{\frac{(-u)L}{2D}}} \tag{5.29}$$

By using the bar in the exponents rather than the solidus, in violation of § 5.2.5, the author has created multiple opportunities for confusion. However, with appropriate substitutions and a modest amount of algebraic manipulation, (5.29) can be rewritten as

$$C = \frac{2(\alpha - \beta)}{\alpha^2 \exp(-z\beta) - \beta^2 \exp(-z\alpha)} \tag{5.30}$$

where $z = uL/2D$, $\alpha = (1+a)$, and $\beta = (1-a)$. Not only does (5.30) clarify the operations in (5.29), but (5.30) also suggests that the important parameter is not a, but rather the combinations $\alpha = (1+a)$ and $\beta = (1-a)$. To test this conjecture we would need experimental data or a theoretical analysis, but the conjecture seems likely because (5.30) shows that C is invariant under an interchange of α and β. No such symmetry is evident in (5.29).

Writers should always display equations in forms that help readers confirm dimensional consistency: the units on the left-hand side (lhs) must be the same as those on the right-hand side (rhs). But checks for dimensional consistency can be made difficult by grouping terms improperly. Consider the following expression for the rate of chemical reaction of succotash in a solution containing hydroxide (OH) ions:

$$\frac{dn_{Suc}}{dt} = (-k)\exp\left(\frac{-(35,000(J/(mol)))}{8.314(J/(molK))T}\right)\left(\frac{S_{Suc0}}{n_{Suc0}^{2/3}} n_{Suc}^{2/3} C_{OH}\right) \tag{5.31}$$

Here n_{Suc} is the number of moles of succotash present at any time t, k is the reaction rate constant in m/sec, T is the temperature in K, S_{Suc0} is the initial surface area of succotash in m^2, n_{Suc0} is the initial number of moles of succotash, and C_{OH} is the OH concentration in mol/m^3.

As is often the case, (5.31) has several problems: the three and four-character subscripts are superfluous, the constant 8.314 J/(mol K) is in fact the universal gas constant R, and the units distract rather than enlighten. But the lesson here is that, by regrouping terms, we can help readers test whether the units on the rhs are consistent with those on the left. Thus we rewrite (5.31) in the form

$$\frac{dn}{dt} = -k\, S_0 C \left(\frac{n}{n_o}\right)^{2/3} \exp\left(\frac{-E}{RT}\right) \qquad (5.32)$$

where $E = 35{,}000$ J/mol and R is the gas constant. Note that the unnecessary subscripts have been removed, and the constant R has been properly identified. Further, in (5.32) the terms have been grouped so the units are easily checked: the argument of exp is dimensionless, as is the ratio (n/n_o), and consequently the units on the rhs are determined by the product (kS_0C). Those units (m/sec $\times$ m^2 $\times$ mol/m^3 = mol/sec) are readily confirmed to be consistent with the units of dn/dt (mol/sec).

5.4 MEANING AND INTERPRETATION

Readers are helped in their struggles to understand equations when writers interpret equations in alternative ways. Interpretations cannot be provided for all equations, but they should be given for all important equations—those that we use repeatedly, or that we take the trouble to derive theoretically, or that we test experimentally. How much interpretation is sufficient? The amount is determined by the complexity of the equation and by the experience of the reader; generally, it is better to offer too much interpretation rather than too little. Even a mathematically sophisticated reader may balk at devoting time to explore the implications of a particular equation. Further, no one interpretation will satisfy all readers, so we should offer alternatives in the hope that any one reader will find at least one version that connects to previous experience. In this section we discuss physical interpretations (§ 5.4.1), mathematical interpretations (§ 5.4.2), and graphical interpretations (§ 5.4.3).

5.4.1 PHYSICAL INTERPRETATIONS

When we seek a physical interpretation for an equation our first impulse is to consider each variable separately. But physical significance rarely resides in individual variables; instead, the important physical meaning is usually attributed to groups of variables. For example, the flow of fluid through pipes is routinely characterized by the dimensionless Reynolds number Re, where

$$Re = \frac{\rho u d}{\mu} \tag{5.33}$$

Here ρ is the density of the fluid, u is its linear velocity, d is the inside diameter of the pipe, and μ is the fluid's viscosity. These four quantities certainly have clear physical meanings, but although I may understand ρ, u, d, and μ separately, I still don't necessarily understand the Reynolds number.

The Reynolds number is important because it provides a quantitative comparison of the forces that support and inhibit flow. Thus Re represents the ratio of inertial forces (measured by $\rho u d$) to viscous forces (measured by μ): inertial forces tend to preserve a flow, while viscous forces tend to impede it. Large values of Re imply inertial flows that cause strong eddy currents, large velocity gradients, and turbulence; low values of Re imply viscous flows with few eddies and gentle velocity gradients. The Reynolds number indicates that we can achieve viscous flow not only by increasing viscosity, but also by decreasing the pipe diameter and the flow rate.

In some instances readers may be helped by writing an equation purely in words. Such *word equations* are often an economical way to convey meaning. To illustrate, here is the balance equation on a bank account:

$$
\begin{bmatrix} \text{change in} \\ \text{accumulation of} \\ \text{funds in account} \end{bmatrix} = \begin{bmatrix} \text{amount} \\ \text{paid} \\ \text{into account} \end{bmatrix} - \begin{bmatrix} \text{amount} \\ \text{withdrawn} \\ \text{from account} \end{bmatrix} \tag{5.34}
$$

$$
+ \begin{bmatrix} \text{amount of} \\ \text{interest paid} \\ \text{into account} \end{bmatrix} - \begin{bmatrix} \text{amount for service} \\ \text{charges paid} \\ \text{out of account} \end{bmatrix}
$$

This is a finite difference equation that applies over a specified duration; to solve for the balance, we would need to know the amount in the account at the start of the relevant duration.

Word equations provide powerful ways to convey simple relations, but they are less useful for showing complicated relations. Moreover, when we use a word equation we forfeit the ease, provided by symbols, of pursuing mathematical manipulations. Thus, word equations should be used sparingly; reserve them for equations that are important yet fairly simple.

Symbolic equations and word equations each offer advantages, but those advantages are lost when the two forms are mixed. Never confuse readers by mixing words and symbols in the same equation; that is, don't create things like this:

$$
S = vk\left(\frac{273.15}{\text{temp}}\right)\left(\frac{\text{atm pres}}{760}\right)\left(\frac{\%N((\text{atm pres})/100)}{\text{sat pres}}\right) \tag{5.35}
$$

Instead, create a viable notation (see § 5.1) and use it.

Besides offering physical interpretations of individual terms or whole equations, we can sometimes help readers understand equations by suggesting how terms or quantities can be measured. Consider the thermal pressure coefficient γ, which is a property of fluids defined by the following partial derivative:

$$\gamma = \left(\frac{\partial P}{\partial T}\right)_V \qquad (5.36)$$

Here P is the fluid pressure, T is its temperature, and V is its volume. To measure γ we could follow this procedure: completely fill a rigid vessel with the fluid; the vessel has volume V, a securely fitted top, and ports fitted with a thermometer and pressure gage for measuring T and P. Now heat the fluid to increase T by a small amount ΔT, and record the corresponding pressure increase ΔP. The ratio $\Delta P/\Delta T$ approximates γ; the approximation improves as ΔT is made smaller. Although such an experiment is rarely done to obtain γ, such an experiment *could* be done and, more to the point, the experiment offers a physical picture that readers can legitimately associate with the abstract derivative in (5.36).

Still another way to help readers is to show how an equation is affected by bounds or limits or other special cases. For example, the law of cosines applies to any triangle,

$$c^2 = a^2 + b^2 - 2ab \cos C \qquad (5.37)$$

where a, b, and c are the lengths of the three sides and C is the angle opposite side c. But when C is a right angle, (5.37) simplifies to the Pythagorean theorem.

As a second example, consider the pressure-volume-temperature (PVT) equation for gases constructed by J. D. van der Waals in his doctoral dissertation of 1873 [4],

$$P = \frac{NRT}{V - Nb} - \frac{aN^2}{V^2} \tag{5.38}$$

Here R is the universal gas constant, N is the number of moles of gas, and the parameters a and b are usually assumed to be constants for a particular substance. This PVT equation was intended to improve on the ideal-gas law, which is only reliable at low densities. Still, the ideal-gas law *is* accurate at low densities, and any more general PVT equation should capture that low-density behavior. And in fact, when the volume V of the container is sufficiently increased with the temperature T and the amount of gas N held constant, the van der Waals equation reduces to the ideal-gas law:

$$\lim_{V \to \text{large}} P = \frac{NRT}{V} \tag{5.39}$$

5.4.2 MATHEMATICAL INTERPRETATIONS

Besides offering physical interpretations, we can also help readers extract meaning from equations by suggesting mathematical interpretations. The most enlightening interpretations seem to be those that reveal patterns, especially patterns that are familiar to readers. In this section we consider three ways to search for patterns: (1) Look for operations that leave the original pattern of the equation unchanged. (2) Look for analogies; that is, look for other phenomena that can be described by the same equation. Readers unfamiliar with your application may recognize the equation when it is placed within a familiar context. (3) Look for ways to transform your equation into alternative forms. Certain groups of readers may find one form more palatable than another.

5.4.2.1 SYMMETRY

When an equation is unchanged as a result of being subjected to a certain operation, then the equation is *symmetric* with respect to that operation. An equation may possess any of several kinds of symmetry, but only the four most common are cited here. Consider an equation in two independent variables and written in the form $F(x, y) = 0$. Then the equation is symmetric under an *inversion in x* when

$$F(-x,y) = F(x, y) \tag{5.40}$$

It is symmetric under a *displacement in x* when

$$F(x + \lambda,y) = F(x, y) \tag{5.41}$$

It is symmetric under a *dilatation in x* when

$$F(\lambda x,y) = F(x, y) \tag{5.42}$$

And it is symmetric under *permutation* when

$$F(y, x) = F(x, y) \tag{5.43}$$

In (5.41) and (5.42) λ is a constant, independent of both x and y. Inversion, displacement, and dilatation symmetries can pertain to either x or y or to both x and y.

As a simple example, the Pythagorean theorem [5]

$$c^2 = a^2 + b^2 \tag{5.44}$$

is symmetric to an inversion of any of the three variables and to permutations of the sides a and b. It is also symmetric under those dilatations in which all three sides are scaled by the same factor λ. However, it is not symmetric under displacements of any side or any combination of sides.

Symmetries in equations usually reflect symmetries in the underlying physical situation, and this is one reason symmetries should be explicitly brought to the attention of readers. Further, if the physical situation contains some symmetry that is not evident in the equation, then it is often worthwhile to recast the equation to bring out the expected symmetry.

Another advantage provided by symmetry is the fundamental Symmetry Principle: All symmetries present in an equation must also be present in its solution. A solution may possess more symmetries than the equation, but never less. If an equation has multiple solutions, then the symmetry principle applies to the entire set of solutions, not to individual solutions [6].

However, symmetries in an equation may be broken if the equation is subjected to auxiliary conditions. These auxiliary conditions include constraints applied to algebraic equations, boundary conditions applied to differential equations, and integration limits. For example, the differential equation

$$\frac{df}{dx} = \frac{f}{x} \tag{5.45}$$

has permutation symmetry ($f \leftrightarrow x$). But this symmetry will persist in the solution only when the limits of integration are the same for both variables. For example, if the limits lead to this,

$$\int_1^F \frac{df}{f} = \int_1^X \frac{dx}{x} \tag{5.46}$$

then the solution is $F = X$, and the symmetry is preserved. But if the limits lead to this,

$$\int_1^F \frac{df}{f} = \int_2^X \frac{dx}{x} \tag{5.47}$$

then the solution is $F = X/2$, and the symmetry is broken.

5.4.2.2 SAME EQUATION, OTHER CONTEXTS

Searches for symmetry are conducted within the confines of the equation itself, though a search may be guided by symmetries in the physical situation. But sometimes other patterns can be found by searching beyond the immediate confines of the equation or even the underlying physical situation. We may look to mathematics to see whether our equation is a particular application of a familiar mathematical generality; or, we may look to other phenomena to see whether the equation's functional form occurs. If we find other contexts in which our equation applies, then we may be justified in attempting to construct analogies that help promote understanding for readers as well as ourselves.

For a first example, consider the problem of creating light of a certain color by mixing three light beams, each having one of the primary colors red R, blue B, or green G. Let r be the amount of light in the red beam R, b the amount in B, and g the amount in G. Then experimentally we find that the color X of the mixed beam is given by

$$X = rR + bB + gG \tag{5.48}$$

Further, if we change the amounts in the primary beams, we create another color Y,

$$Y = r'R + b'B + g'G \tag{5.49}$$

and if we mix beams X and Y, we obtain experimentally yet another color Z, where

$$Z = (r + r')R + (b + b')B + (g + g')G \qquad (5.50)$$

These equations take a familiar pattern: they have the structure of vectors. In particular, (5.50) is the vector sum of (5.48) and (5.49), with the basis vectors represented by R, B, G and the "lengths" of the components given by r, b, and g. Thus problems in mixing light devolve to problems in vector algebra, and any problem associated with creating light of a particular color can be solved using the established machinery of vector analysis [7].

For a second example, we turn from purely mathematical connections to patterns that persist over different, apparently unrelated phenomena. We consider the expression that describes how a population increases with time. Let N represent the number of individuals in a population at time t; then in an unlimited environment the rate of change of N is proportional to N itself,

$$\frac{dN}{dt} = kN \qquad (5.51)$$

where k is a constant. The exponential is a function whose derivative is proportional to itself, so the solution to (5.51) can be expressed as the growth law,

$$N(t) = N_o \, e^{kt} \qquad (5.52)$$

where N_o is the number present at the initial time $t = 0$. What we want to emphasize is that the patterns in (5.51) and (5.52) occur in many settings.

Application 1. Equations (5.51) and (5.52) apply to the compounding of funds in interest-bearing accounts. Let P_o be the amount of principal initially placed in an account that earns $r\%$ per year. If no withdrawals are made, then after t years the amount in the account P is given by

$$P(t) = P_O \, e^{(rt)/100} \tag{5.53}$$

provided t is greater than about five years.

Application 2. Equations (5.51) and (5.52) describe how the density of air varies in a stagnant constant-temperature atmosphere. Let ρ_0 be the atmospheric density at the planet's surface, then the density ρ at any elevation h is

$$\rho(h) = \rho_O \, e^{-ch} \tag{5.54}$$

where c is a constant. The negative sign indicates that the density decreases as we move to higher altitudes. The earth's atmosphere only approximately obeys (5.54) because the atmosphere is neither stagnant nor at the same temperature at all elevations.

Application 3. Consider an object, initially at temperature T_0, placed in an environment that is at a cooler temperature T_e. According to a law formulated by Newton, the rate of cooling of the object will be proportional to the temperature difference, $\Delta T = T - T_e$. Then analogous to (5.51) and (5.52), we have

$$\Delta T = \Delta T_O \, e^{-\alpha t} \tag{5.55}$$

where α is a constant and $\Delta T_0 = T_0 - T_e$. So from the initial temperature T_0, the temperature of the object exponentially cools to that of its environment.

Application 4. At time t_0 a substance contains N_0 atoms of a radioactive isotope. The rate of radioactive decay proceeds in proportion to the number of atoms N, so at any time t after t_0, the number of radioactive atoms remaining is given by

$$N(t) = N_O \, e^{-kt} \tag{5.56}$$

where k is a rate constant. The half-life for the isotope is the time at which the number $N(t)$ has fallen to half the original value N_0.

These four examples are not by any means all the known situations in which the patterns (5.51) and (5.52) apply, but they are sufficient to illustrate our point: often apparently different phenomena can be described by the same or similar equations, and readers may be helped by noting when such similarities occur. When the similarities are strong, then we may obtain insight by seeking explanations for those similarities or by exploiting the implied analogies.

5.4.2.3 SAME CONTEXT, OTHER EQUATIONS

In previous subsections we have emphasized how readers may be helped when a writer shows how an important equation can be interpreted in either physical or mathematical terms. In this subsection we consider helping readers by transforming an equation into other forms. By displaying alternative but equivalent forms, we may awaken some readers to meaning that might otherwise be overlooked, and we may help other readers see how an equation might apply in other situations.

As a first example, consider an arbitrary plane triangle of sides a, b, c, and altitude h. The area A of this triangle is conventionally computed from

$$A = \frac{bh}{2} \tag{5.57}$$

Thus the area of any triangle is half the area of a rectangle whose width is b and whose height is h. To use (5.57) we must determine the altitude h, which requires us to construct a right angle because h is perpendicular to b. However, the construction or measurement of angles can be avoided if we use this alternative to (5.57), which involves the semiperimeter $s = (a + b + c)/2$,

$$A^2 = s(s-a)(s-b)(s-c) \qquad (5.58)$$

The alternative (5.58) is usually attributed to Heron of Alexandria [8], who is thought to have lived in the first century A.D. Heron's formula is particularly useful to surveyors; thus, to determine the area of a plot of land, we need only divide the plot into any convenient number of contiguous triangles, measure the lengths of all sides, and repeatedly apply (5.58).

As a second example, consider Newton's law for the gravitational force F acting between two bodies of masses M and m, with the centers of mass separated by a distance r,

$$F = -G\frac{Mm}{r^2} \qquad (5.59)$$

The value of the gravitational constant G is obtained from experiment. According to (5.59) the force decreases as the square of the separation; so, if the distance between two bodies is doubled, then the gravitational force is reduced by a factor of four.

Although (5.59) may be familiar to many readers, some readers may be helped if we offer an alternative. For example, gravity can be described not only in terms of a force but also in terms of an energy. Thus, let $U(r)$ represent the gravitational potential energy that exists at a distance r from the center of a body having mass M. When a second body of mass m is situated at r, the potential energy per unit mass of m is given by

$$\frac{U(r)}{m} = -\frac{GM}{r} \qquad (5.60)$$

where r is the distance between the centers of the two bodies.

The two descriptions of gravity (5.59) and (5.60) are equivalent. To show this, we recall that a conservative force equals the negative r-derivative of the potential energy function,

$$F = -\frac{dU}{dr} \tag{5.61}$$

Substituting (5.60) into (5.61) and taking the derivative reproduces Newton's form (5.59).

Equations (5.59) and (5.60) illustrate the distinction between Newtonian and Hamiltonian dynamics: in Newtonian dynamics motion is caused by forces acting between bodies, but in Hamiltonian dynamics motion is a consequence of the conservation of energy. The Newtonian and Hamiltonian views of classical mechanics are entirely equivalent, but some readers may prefer one interpretation over the other. Moreover, in a particular situation one form or the other may simplify an analysis or a calculation. As writers we should give readers opportunities for understanding equations by offering alternative interpretations, whenever alternatives are available or can be contrived.

5.4.3 GRAPHICAL INTERPRETATIONS

In addition to the physical and mathematical alternatives suggested in previous sections, we can also interpret equations using plots and charts. For example, by plotting individual terms in an equation we can show how each term contributes to the total effect. Further, plots can be used to extract and present meaning that is difficult to convey in any other way—remember the old adage: a word is only worth one millipicture. Thus plots can be used to show comparisons, reveal patterns, illustrate complexity, and present numerical solutions when analytic solutions are unobtainable. We do not illustrate all these uses here; instead, we are content to emphasize that some apparently simple equations can embody relations that are not really simple.

As an example, consider superimposing three sine waves,

$$T = \sin\theta + \sin a\theta + \sin b\theta \tag{5.62}$$

All three waves have the same amplitude, but the three have slightly different periods, as indicated by the factors a and b. An example is shown in Figure 5.1; the top part of the figure shows the three waves, and the bottom part shows their sum (5.62). Even though the waves are related in a simple way, their combination would be impossible to visualize without the figure. Figures such as (5.1) suggest how ocean waves can combine to cause high rollers interspersed by brief periods of calm.

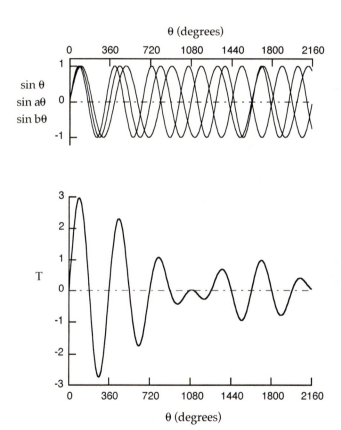

Figure 5.1 *(top)* Three sine waves (sin θ, sin $a\theta$, sin $b\theta$) that appear on the rhs of (5.62), with $a = 1.108$ and $b = 0.89$. *(bottom)* Superposition of the three waves (5.62).

Complexities embedded in an equation may remain suppressed until the value of a controlling parameter reaches some critical value. That is, a single equation may describe several different behaviors depending on the values of certain parameters. In such situations a plot is usually the best way to bring those differences to the reader's attention. Some equations may be deceptively simple: they can hide a wealth of behavior that is best communicated in graphical form.

5.5 SUMMARY

Every technical communication should probe, explain, or at least document relations—relations between pieces of equipment, between inputs and outputs, between processes, between causes and effects, and between ideas. Relations among ideas can often be most effectively and economically presented via equations. But the power and economy of equations will thwart the efforts of some readers to comprehend, and so writers should aim to present equations that serve the reader.

To achieve effective equations, we must edit equations with the same care that we give to text. In an effective equation every symbol is carefully placed so that readers may readily grasp important relations without being distracted by less important details. Further, an effective equation is constructed from a viable notation, with terms grouped in meaningful ways, and it possesses a transparent structure, unencumbered by ambiguities, redundancies, and unnecessary symbols.

To help readers appreciate important equations, we should supplement them with additional commentary, alternative equations, or graphical interpretations. These supplemental devices will aid not only those readers who are inexperienced in decoding equations, but also those many readers who cannot devote the time needed to explore an equation's intricacies and ramifications. These supplements should not be treated as secondary material: we should never rely *exclusively* on equations to convey meaning. Rather, equations should be balanced with other explanatory devices—text, tables, and figures. Neither should we use equations promiscuously; instead, we should use them judiciously, clearly stating their meanings, limitations, and implications. Otherwise some readers will view our writing as obscure, or confused, or even mystical.

EXERCISES

5.1 For each of the following, create a meaningful notation and use your notation to express each relation as an equation:
  (a) The surface area of an enclosed right cylinder is twice pi times the square of the radius added to twice pi times the radius times the height.
  (b) Stirling's approximation for the factorials of large integers: the natural log of the factorial is approximately the integer subtracted from the integer times its natural log.
  (c) The sine of an angle is the same as the cosine of its complement.
  (d) The course grade is a weighted average of homework, midterm exam, term paper, and final exam. The midterm exam and term paper each have twice the weight of homework, while the final exam has three times the weight of homework.
  (e) Genius is 90% perspiration plus 10% inspiration.

5.2 Rewrite the following equations using the rules in § 5.2. If the order of operations is ambiguous, multiplication and division take precedence over addition and subtraction.

(a) $\ln(1 + x) = x(1 - x/2 + x^2/3 - x^3/4 + \ldots)$

(b) $x = [(-b)\{b \times b - (4 \cdot c \cdot a)\}^{1/2}]/\{2 \bullet a\}$

(c) $\int \frac{(a + bx)^{-1}}{a + bx}\, dx = -[\{1/b\}[a + (bx)]^{-1}]$

(d) $\tan 3x = (3\tan x)/(1 - 3[\tan x]^2) - (\tan x[\tan x]^2)/\{1 - 3\tan x \tan x\}$

(e) $y = ([\pi]^{-0.5}/2^{1/2})e^{\frac{-x \times x}{2}}$

(f) $T_{centi} + 153 = \dfrac{5T_{Fahr}}{9} + 7/9$

(g) $\text{radius} = \left[\dfrac{1}{s}\right]\left(\dfrac{s(s-a))(s-b)}{(s-c)^{-1}}\right)^{0.5}$

(h) $\text{area} = \left(\dfrac{1}{r^{-1}}\right)r\dfrac{\{\theta - \sin\theta\}}{1/0.5}$

5.3 Check whether the following equations are dimensionally consistent. The symbols have these dimensions: N(moles), P(pressure), T(temperature), V(volume), b(volume/mole), v(volume/mole), ρ(mole/volume), R(pressure × volume/ mole) = R(energy/mole), with y and Z both dimensionless.

(a) $P = \rho RT$

(b) $Pv = NRT$

(c) $y = \exp(P/(RT))$

(d) $Z = 1 + b\rho$

(e) $P = \dfrac{RT}{V - b}$

(f) $v = \dfrac{RT}{P} + \dfrac{bRT}{Pv}$

5.4 Show whether the following are symmetric under (i) inversions of x, (ii) displacements in x, (iii) dilatations in x, and (iv) permutations of x and y:

(a) $y = mx + b$ (b) $y = ax^2$ (c) $r = \sqrt{x^2 + y^2}$

(d) $x + y = 1$ (e) $x - y = 1$ (f) $\dfrac{x}{y} = 4x$

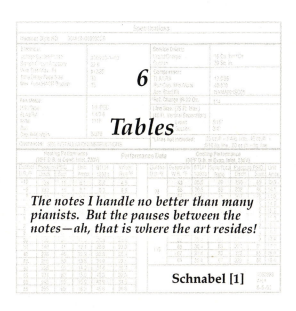

6

Tables

*The notes I handle no better than many
pianists. But the pauses between the
notes—ah, that is where the art resides!*

Schnabel [1]

Whenever we generate many numbers, whether by calculation or by experiment, we invariably reach a point at which the data must be reduced to coherent and accessible forms. Such forms are usually realized as tables. Tables help us organize information into economical units; they help make comparisons; they reveal trends and anomalies; they clarify presentations and lines of reasoning. Moreover tables can serve as bases for further analyses [2]. To create a table we must select the data to be presented, organize the data into meaningful patterns, and document the presentation using such devices as captions, headings, and footnotes. Of these three steps, the first—selecting the data—is a problem peculiar to a particular experimental or computational situation and is beyond the scope of this book. So in this chapter we focus on the second and third steps: organizing the chosen data into tables and documenting the presentation. As with all aspects of communication, each table must be designed with its intended use in mind and then edited to ensure that its intended effect is achieved.

6.1 KINDS OF TABLES

Tables may be simple to construct and straightforward to read, or they may be complicated by many interrelated variables. Complicated tables may require effort to decipher, and yet complicated tables can be effective. The point is that tables should be complicated because the data are complicated, not because the data are poorly organized. Simple data should appear in simple tables. In this section we describe four kinds of simple tables: unilateral and bilateral forms, matrix tables, and tables without numbers.

6.1.1 UNILATERAL TABLES

By a *unilateral table* we mean one that contains a single independent variable; typically, values of the independent variable occupy the left-most column. The independent variable may be a single quantity cited at a sequence of values, or it may be a class of things cited by members of the class. The table may contain one or more dependent variables, which are identified in column headings across the top of the table; their values constitute the body of the table. Thus values of the dependent variables are compared by reading only in the vertical direction—unilaterally.

An example of a simple unilateral table is given in Table 6.1, which shows the melting and boiling points for some hydrides from group VI of the periodic table. Table 6.1 suggests that water is an unusual substance: although it has a low molecular weight, water has the highest melting and boiling points of any of the group VI hydrides. Many of water's anomalous properties are caused by the strong hydrogen bonding that occurs among its molecules; thus, in addition to the high melting temperature shown in Table 6.1, water expands on freezing, so ice floats. Consequently, as Atkins has remarked elsewhere [3], hydrogen bonding was responsible for the sinking of the *R. M. S. Titanic.*

Table 6.1
Melting Point (Mpt) and Boiling Point (Bpt) of
Hydrides from Group VI of the Periodic Table [4]

Substance	Formula	Mol Wt	Mpt (°C)	Bpt (°C)
Water	H_2O	18	0	100
Hydrogen sulfide	H_2S	34	–82	–61
Hydrogen selenide	H_2Se	81	–61	–42
Hydrogen telluride	H_2Te	130	–51	–4

Table 6.1 represents a simple unilateral table; more complex unilateral tables occur when one or more dependent variables subdivide into categories. An example is shown in Table 6.2, which presents certain features of the nine planets of the solar system. In this table the distances to the sun are cited at their minimum, mean, and maximum values, and these are indicated by the *decked heading* over the columns. Note that all values in Table 6.2 are quoted relative to those of the Earth; such relative values often use less space than absolute ones, and they may be more meaningful to most readers. Thus, the diameter of Mars is about half that of Earth; this will be appreciated by more readers than the statement that Mars has a diameter of 6760 km.

6.1.2 BILATERAL TABLES

By a *bilateral* table we mean one that contains two independent variables; values of one independent variable are listed in the first column, and values of the other are listed in the column headings across the top. Thus changes in the one or more dependent variables can be read both horizontally and vertically—

Table 6.2
Distances, Periods, and Diameters of the Planets [5]
Abbreviations in headings are identified in the footnotes.

Planet	Distance from Sun			Period		Equa Dia
	Min	Mn	Max	Revo	Rota	
Mercury	0.3	0.39	0.46	0.24	59	0.38
Venus	0.71	0.72	0.73	0.62	243	0.95
Earth	0.98	1.†	1.01	1.*	1.§	1.‡
Mars	1.38	1.52	1.66	1.9	1.03	0.53
Jupiter	4.94	5.2	5.44	11.9	0.41	11.3
Saturn	9.0	9.5	10.0	29.5	0.43	9.46
Uranus	18.2	19.2	20.0	84	0.72	4.0
Neptune	29.7	30.0	30.2	165	0.67	3.9
Pluto	29.5	39.4	49.2	248	6.4	0.18

† Earth's mean (Mn) distance from sun $\quad = 1.5(10^8)$ km
* period of revolution (Revo) around sun $= 365.3$ days
§ period of rotation (Rota) around axis $\quad = 23.93$ hours
‡ equatorial diameter (Equa Dia) $\quad\quad = 12{,}756$ km

bilaterally. An example appears in Table 6.3, which shows mean life expectancies for the population of Sweden. These data are cited because demographic records in Sweden extend over longer periods than those of most other countries. The life expectancies for peoples of Western Europe and North America are expected to be similar to those in Table 6.3.

Table 6.3 shows that life expectancy depends on the year of birth and on current age. Thus, as in any bilateral table, patterns can be found by reading either horizontally across columns or

Table 6.3
Mean Life Expectancy (years) in Sweden [6]

Date	From birth	From age 60	From age 80
1755-76	34.4	12.7	4.4
1856-60	42.3	13.6	4.0
1936-40	65.6	16.8	5.4
1971-75	74.9	19.5	6.7

vertically over rows. The columns document the historical rise in life expectancy; in particular, over the 220 years from 1755 to 1975 the life expectancy from birth has more than doubled. Columns 3 and 4 indicate that the life expectancy from later ages has increased by about 50%. The rows in the table show that chances for a long life increase with age. Thus of the people born in 1975, half could expect to reach age 75; but of those who were already 60 in 1975, half could expect to reach age 80. Nothing succeeds like success [7].

Table 6.3 illustrates a simple bilateral table containing only one dependent variable. When more dependent variables are included, the table must be designed to clearly communicate relations among the dependent and independent variables. A common example is provided by a steam table, in which volumes, enthalpies, and entropies of steam are presented as functions of both temperature and pressure.

6.1.3 MATRIX TABLES

When we have members of a group of things, we often want to know how pairs of group members are related or are correlated with one another. More generally, we may have property or parameter values A_{ij} that apply to the *ij*-pair of members. Such pairwise relations or values can be displayed as a *matrix* table. In such a table the group members are presented as both the first column and as column headings. The body of the table contains values of the properties A_{ij}.

To illustrate, we use an empirical correlation for the gas-liquid critical temperatures T_{cm} of fluid mixtures [8],

$$T_{cm} = \sum_{i=1}^{n} \left(\frac{x_i T_{ci}}{\sum_{\substack{j \neq i}}^{n} A_{ij} x_j} \right) \tag{6.1}$$

Here n is the number of components in the mixture, T_{ci} is the critical temperature of pure component i, x_i is the mole fraction of i, and the A_{ij} are empirical parameters for the ij-pair of components. In this correlation no contribution is obtained from pairs formed by the same component; thus, the parameters A_{ii} are undefined. Values of the A_{ij} parameters can be presented in a matrix table, such as that in Table 6.4, which applies to mixtures of ethane, propane, butane, and pentane ($n = 4$).

In some situations the parameters A_{ij} are symmetric under interchange of labels, that is, $A_{ji} = A_{ij}$. Then the matrix table is symmetric about its diagonal elements, and only one triangular half of the table need be displayed. Examples include mileage tables given on maps and atlases, as in Table 6.5. In practice, the

Table 6.4
Values of the Coefficients A_{ij} in Equation (6.1) for Mixtures
Containing Ethane, Propane, Butane, and Pentane [8]

i	Fluid	j 1 Ethane	2 Propane	3 Butane	4 Pentane
1	Ethane	...	0.966	0.849	0.813
2	Propane	0.986	...	1.017	0.914
3	Butane	0.960	0.973	...	1.059
4	Pentane	0.884	0.986	0.955	...

Table 6.5
Road Miles Between Selected Cities [9]

	Boston	Denver	LA	Miami	DC
Boston	...	1998	3017	1520	448
Denver	...	...	1031	2107	1616
LA	...	...	...	2716	2646
Miami	...	...	...	...	1057
DC	...	...	...	...	...

last row in Table 6.5 would not normally be displayed; it is shown here for pedagogical reasons.

6.1.4 NONNUMERIC TABLES

In addition to presenting numerical values, tables can also be used to organize and display nonnumerical information. The possible applications include citing steps in a procedure, steps in a logical argument, and descriptions of members of a class. A nonnumeric table also provides an economical way to present a family of related equations. Most nonnumeric tables take the unilateral form; an example appears in Table 6.6.

6.2 MECHANICS OF PRESENTATION

Tables should merely present facts; discussion and interpretation of those facts should be presented in the text. Thus, as a collection of facts, a table should be complete and able to stand alone, separate from the text. To meet this requirement, a table must be carefully organized and completely documented. The basic guidelines of documentation are cited in this section [10].

Table 6.6

A Bestiary of Figures of Speech [11]

Name	Definition	Example
Anadiplosis	using a previous ending as a beginning	*Strive for clarity, for clarity resolves many issues of style.*
Anaphora	repeated beginnings	*Perhaps you have heard this before. Perhaps you remember.*
Antithesis	repeated in the negative	*The proof is wrong; it is certainly not valid.*
Asterismos	using unneeded words to draw attention to what follows	*Confusion often arises from this, an inability to resolve contradictions.*
Asyndeton	omitting a conjunction	*The presentation was brief, spirited, superficial.*
Epistrophe	repeated endings	*To write well, read well.*
Pleonasm	using superfluous words	*Try, try again.*
Polyptoton	repeating a word or root but in a different grammatical form	*Common sense is not common. (Voltaire)*
Polysyndeton	using unneeded conjunctions	*The text was long and hard and dull.*
Scesis onomaton	omitting all verbs	*This sentence no verb.*
Zeugma	omitting a verb(s) so that a remaining verb applies to more than one clause	*He skips rope daily and lunch occasionally.*

6.2.1 TABLE NUMBERS

Each table should be numbered and explicitly cited by number in the text; moreover, each table should appear immediately following its first citation. If a document contains only one table then no number is needed, but the table should still be cited in the text. If during editing you find that a table has not been cited or discussed, then perhaps the table is unnecessary; consider moving it to an appendix or eliminating it altogether.

6.2.2 TITLES

The contents of a table should be identified in a title that is meaningful but not voluminous. Titles should be capitalized, either in headline or in sentence style, with the same style used for all tables in a document. (In headline style, all important words are capitalized, as in headlines of newspapers. Unimportant words include prepositions and conjunctions.) To give units or values that apply to all entries in a table, subtitles can be used. Subtitles should start on a line separate from the title.

6.2.3 SEPARATORS

To achieve visual separations use white space rather than grids or vertical rules. Most tables need only three horizontal rules: above and below the column headings and below the body. If the body subdivides, the subdivisions can be indicated by a thin horizontal rule; however, an extra blank line often separates just as well. When a heading is decked, as in Table 6.2, insert a thin horizontal rule between the upper *spanner* heading and the lower column headings. This horizontal rule should be exactly as wide as the spanned columns.

6.2.4 HEADINGS

Column headings are usually singular, and they usually start with a capital letter. In unilateral tables the heading of the first column can be omitted when the category is obvious or has been stated in the title. Otherwise, each heading should include the units and any scale factors that apply to entries in that column.

Scale factors in headings can be confusing because readers may not realize whether entries should be multiplied or divided by the factor. To help forestall confusion, adhere to the following convention: if entries have been multiplied by a factor, place the factor in parentheses in the heading; if entries have been divided by a factor, precede the factor by a solidus. Here is one way to remember how scale factors apply: construct an equation that represents an equality between a column entry and the column heading; this interpretation is illustrated in Table 6.7. If you are not confident that readers will correctly interpret scale factors, give an example in a footnote.

Table 6.7
How to Interpret Scale Factors in Column Headings

	Example Headings	
	Mass $m(g)(100)$	Volume $V(cc)/100$
Original entry in table	2.6	2.6
Meaning of heading	Value of m has been multiplied by 100	Value of V has been divided by 100
Equation to interpret entry	$m(g) \times 100 = 2.6$	$V(cc)/100 = 2.6$
Correct value	$m = 0.026$ g	$V = 260$ cc

6.2.5 COLUMN ENTRIES

All entries in a column should be aligned on their decimal points, and the correct number of significant figures should be used for each entry. In most tables, all entries in a column should have the same number of significant figures. Precede all fractions with a leading zero; that is, write 0.25, not .25. In non-numeric tables short entries can be aligned vertically on the column center, as in the first column of Table 6.6. Otherwise, left justify nonnumeric entries, as in the second column of Table 6.6.

Choose the units and scale factors for columns so the magnitudes of entries are readily assimilated by readers; usually magnitudes of order unity are preferred. When powers of ten are needed, use proper scientific notation (6.023×10^{23}), not computer jargon (6.023e23 or 6.023**23). Do not create a row or column whose entries are all the same; instead, cite common entries once, either in a subtitle or in a footnote.

6.2.6 FOOTNOTES

Footnotes should appear below the body and justified with the left of the table, as in Table 6.2. For footnote marks, symbols (*, †, ‡ , §, ¶) are preferred over numerals, so as to avoid possible confusion with exponents. A footnote applies to all levels subordinate to that having the reference mark; thus, if a mark appears on a column heading, then the footnote applies to all entries in that column. Likewise, if a reference mark is applied to the title, then the footnote applies to the entire table.

6.3 EFFECTIVE DESIGN

To be effective a table must be organized so that the presentation is logical and economical. Moreover, the structure of a table should be transparent; that is, the structure should not intervene between the reader and the data. A table's structure should help the reader see the data, see extremes in the data, and see how the data respond to changes in the independent variables. When the data are few and simply related, then a table may be readily constructed. But when many numbers are to be tabulated or the relations among the numbers are complicated, then the design of a table may require substantial effort. In such situations, several attempts may be needed before a successful table is achieved.

In this section we critique a few poorly prepared tables and show how they can be improved. The weak examples shown here could have been created by anybody—as first drafts. The lesson is that we should rarely be satisfied with first drafts.

6.3.1 EDIT TO IMPROVE ORGANIZATION

In Table 6.8a we show data obtained for calibrating a meter that monitors the volumetric flow rate of water through a pipe. The calibration data were obtained using a bucket, scales, and stop-watch. We immediately see some minor discrepancies; for

Table 6.8a
Calibration of a Flow Meter

Run No.	Initial Weight (lbs)	Final Weight (lbs)	Elapsed Time (sec)	Meter Reading (gpm)	Measured Flow Rate (gpm)
1	15	215	417	3.5	3.449
2	5	205	197	7.3	7.302
3	10	210	133	10.8	10.816
4	15	215	113	12.6	12.729
5	15	215	96	14.6	14.984

example, a horizontal rule should appear between body and column headings, and the entries in the last two columns are not properly aligned on their decimal points. Further, the numbers of significant figures in the last column are inconsistent with those for the measured weights and times. These discrepancies are corrected in the revision presented in Table 6.8b.

But more importantly, Table 6.8a could be better organized to help readers more easily see relations between columns. Thus, in the revision we use decked heads to group the initial and final weights and to group both sets of flow rates. Note that these groupings are reinforced by using nonuniform spacing between columns: white space in tables can be used to emphasize the organization. Note also that in Table 6.8b we have reversed the order of the last two columns; the measured flow rates were obtained from the weights and times in the three previous columns, and so by keeping those four columns close together, we emphasize their interdependence.

Table 6.8b

Revision of Table 6.8a: Calibration of a Flow Meter

Run No.	Weight		Elapsed Time (s)	Vol Flow Rate	
	Initial (lbs)	Final (lbs)		Meas'd (gpm)	Meter (gpm)
1	15	215	417	3.45	3.5
2	5	205	197	7.30	7.3
3	10	210	133	10.8	10.8
4	15	215	113	12.7	12.6
5	15	215	96	15.0	14.6

6.3.2 EDIT TO ACHIEVE ECONOMY

The economy of a presentation can be improved by removing redundancies. An example is offered in Table 6.9a, which lists the amounts of components loaded into a chemical reactor at the start of different experimental runs. This table contains redundant rows and an unnecessary column. Eliminating those reduces the structure to the simpler form contained in Table 6.9b. Further, the vertical rules in Table 6.9a are unnecessary: white space separates columns without distracting readers. That is, vertical rules draw attention away from the data to the rules themselves; this is undesirable, since it is the data that should claim a reader's attention.

Table 6.9a
Amounts of Reactants Loaded into Chemical Reactor

Run No.	Mass of Reactant A (kg)	Volume of Water (l)	Volume of Reactant B (l)
5	5.0	145	4.85
6	5.0	145	4.85
8	5.0	145	4.85
1	10.0	145	9.70
2	10.0	145	9.70
7	10.0	145	9.70
3	20.0	145	19.40
4	20.0	145	19.40
9	20.0	145	19.40

Table 6.9b
Revision of Table 6.9a:
Amounts of Reactants Loaded into Chemical Reactor
In each run the reactor was initially loaded with 145 liters of water.

Run No.	Mass of Reactant A (kg)	Volume of Reactant B (l)
5, 6, 8	5.0	4.85
1, 2, 7	10.0	9.70
3, 4, 9	20.0	19.4

6.3.3 EDIT TO ACHIEVE CLARITY

In Table 6.10a we show heat capacities C for certain binary mixtures at different compositions and temperatures. But the table is so poorly organized that the values of C are difficult to distinguish. In fact, because of the poor organization combined with the distracting grids and redundant citations of units, any reader could be forgiven for failing to find anything instructive in this table.

Since these heat capacities depend on two variables, concentration and temperature, we revised Table 6.10a into the bilateral form shown in Table 6.10b. The revised table makes clear that the nine C-values can be grouped according to temperature (vertical) or according to concentration (horizontal). Moreover, Table 6.10b reveals that C increases with temperature but it decreases with increasing concentration of component A. These trends are obscured in the original Table 6.10a.

Table 6.10a

Heat Capacities of Binary Mixtures of Components A and B

Amt. of A	Heat capacity for temperature range		
8.3 wt.%	(29 to 43°C) J/g K	(43 to 57°C) J/g K	(57 to 71°C) J/g K
	3.30	3.54	3.72
4.4 wt.%	(30 to 43°C) J/g K	(43 to 58°C) J/g K	(58 to 71°C) J/g K
	3.65	3.72	4.02
14.8 wt.%	(27 to 40°C) J/g K	(40 to 53°C) J/g K	(53 to 66°C) J/g K
	3.12	3.37	3.50

Table 6.10b

Revision of Table 6.10a:

Heat Capacities C for Binary Mixtures of A and B

Amt of A wt.%	Low Temperatures		Mid Temperatures		High Temperatures	
	Range (°C)	C (J/g K)	Range (°C)	C (J/g K)	Range (°C)	C (J/g K)
4.4	30-43	3.65	43-58	3.72	58-71	4.02
8.3	29-43	3.30	43-57	3.54	57-71	3.72
14.8	27-40	3.12	40-53	3.37	53-66	3.50

6.3.4 EDIT TO MAKE YOUR POINT

The organization of a table not only affects the clarity of the presentation, but it also influences the patterns seen by readers. Thus Table 6.10b is more effective than Table 6.10a because it allows readers to see trends with changes in both composition and temperature. Often the writer must edit a table through several versions before the most important trends are clarified. To say this another way, two (or more) versions of the same table may be equally legitimate and effective, but the two versions may emphasize different information. Then we present the version that supports the point we are trying to convey.

As an example, consider Table 6.11a which contains the raw data that Lord Rayleigh collected during his experimental studies of the density of nitrogen. The organization of Table 6.11a emphasizes the source of the nitrogen, but the table obscures any pattern in the measured masses. However, when Table 6.11a is rearranged as in Table 6.11b, then a consistent pattern emerges: the nitrogen samples from air were 0.5% heavier than the nitrogen samples obtained by chemical reactions. A dogged search led Rayleigh to conclude that the discrepancy was caused by an unknown substance in air. This new substance Rayleigh and his colleague William Ramsay isolated and named—argon. For this discovery, motivated by his dissatisfaction with a 0.5% discrepancy, Rayleigh was awarded a Nobel Prize.

Taken out of context, Tables 6.11a and 6.11b are both effective; they merely emphasize different aspects of the data. But within the context of trying to understand the data, and trying to convey that understanding, Table 6.11b is a more effective form than Table 6.11a. Editing tables is typically motivated by concern for the reader, but the editing process may also help the writer see new patterns.

Table 6.11a
Rayleigh's Measurements for Determining
the Density of Nitrogen [12]

Date	Mass of Nitrogen Sample (g)	Source of Nitrogen†
29 Nov 1893	2.30143	NO
2 Dec	2.2989	NO
5 Dec	2.29816	NO
6 Dec	2.30182	NO
12 Dec	2.31017	Air
14 Dec	2.30986	Air
19 Dec	2.3101	Air
22 Dec	2.31001	Air
26 Dec	2.29869	N_2O
28 Dec 93	2.2994	N_2O
9 Jan 94	2.29849	NH_4NO_2
13 Jan	2.29889	NH_4NO_2
27 Jan	2.31024	Air
30 Jan	2.3101	Air
1 Feb 1894	2.31028	Air

† NO = nitric oxide, N_2O = nitrous oxide,
NH_4NO_2 = ammonium nitrite

Table 6.11b
Revision of Table 6.11a:
Rayleigh's Measurements for Determining
the Density of Nitrogen [12]

Date	Mass of Nitrogen Sample (g)	
	from chemical reaction	separated from air
29 Nov 1893	2.30143	
2 Dec	2.2989	
5 Dec	2.29816	
6 Dec	2.30182	
12 Dec		2.31017
14 Dec		2.30986
19 Dec.		2.3101
22 Dec		2.31001
26 Dec	2.29869	
28 Dec 1893	2.2994	
9 Jan 1894	2.29849	
13 Jan	2.29889	
27 Jan		2.31024
30 Jan		2.3101
1 Feb 1894		2.31028
average	2.29947	2.31011

6.4 SUMMARY

Many writers seem to devote more effort to text, equations, and figures than they devote to tables. If this observation is generally true, then it is unfortunate, because a properly executed table can be a powerful and direct way to communicate. It may be that a table's effectiveness belies the difficulties encountered in its creation. The structure of an effective table is unobtrusive—the emphasis is on the data, not on the way the data are presented. This is as it should be. But effective tables are usually products of much thought and effort; they rarely spring spontaneously from the minds of writers.

The theme of this chapter is that tables should be designed and edited with the same care as is given to other aspects of technical communication. Poorly executed tables frustrate readers, while properly executed tables can help readers receive your message more readily. Whenever you must explain complicated material or describe trends in data or reveal anomalies in results, consider using a table to organize the material and to keep the discussion focussed on the important points. For not only can tables help make reading less trying, but in addition effective tables can ease the labor of writing.

EXERCISES

6.1 Here are energy densities, in MJ/kg, for common fuels (1 MJ = 1 megajoule = 10^6 J): gasoline, 47; ethanol, 30; air-dried wood, 15; hydrogen, 114; bituminous coal, 28; plant oils, 38; lignites, 19; natural gas, 35; crude oil, 43. Create a table for these data and justify the order in which you arrange the entries in your table. (Data from V. Smil [13].)

6.2 Animals moving through fluids (such as air and water) have Reynolds numbers (Re; see § 5.4.1) that are proportional to speed times body size. Here are some representative values: duck flying at 20 m/s, Re = $3(10^5)$; small flying insect, Re = 30; whale swimming at 10 m/s, Re = $3(10^8)$; invertebrate larva swimming at 1 mm/s, Re = 0.3; dragonfly flying at 7 m/s, Re = $3(10^4)$; sea urchin sperm swimming at 0.2 mm/s, Re = 0.03; tuna swimming at 10 m/s, Re = $3(10^7)$. Create a table for these data and justify the order in which you arrange the entries in your table. (Data from S. Vogel [14].)

6.3 Saturated liquid water has the following properties (u in J/g; v in cc/g): when u = 42, v = 1.000, then T and P are 10°C, 1.23 kPa; when u =100.6, v = 1.003, then T and P are 24°C, 2.98 kPa; u = 200.9, v = 1.011, then T and P are 48°C, 11.2 kPa; u = 301.3, v = 1.024, then T and P are 72°C, 34 kPa; u = 419, v = 1.044, then T and P are 100°C, 101.3 kPa. Make a table for these data in which P (bar) is the independent variable, temperatures are given in both °C and °F, and density (ρ in mol/cc), u, and v are included.

6.4 For liquid-liquid equilibrium between aqueous and organic layers containing water, acetone, and trichloroethane (TCE), the following data are available. At 20°C: when the aqueous layer contains 6 wt% acetone, 0.5% TCE, then the organic layer contains 8.8% acetone and 0.3% water; when the organic layer contains 43% acetone, 3% water, then the aqueous layer contains 31% acetone, 1% TCE. At 30°C: when the organic layer contains 60% acetone, 13% water, then the aqueous layer contains 52% acetone, 6.5% TCE; when the aqueous layer contains 36 wt% acetone, 1.6% TCE, then the organic layer contains 48% acetone and 4.3% water. Create a table for these data in which T is independent and each row presents the weight percentages of all three components in both phases.

6.5 Nine runs were performed on a chemical reactor with the following loadings of reactants A and B (m_a and m_b in kg) and volume of water (v in liters): run 5, $m_a = 5$, $m_b = 4.8$, v = 145; run 4, $m_a = 10$, $m_b = 9.7$, v = 145; run 1, $m_a = 10$, $m_b = 9.7$, v = 145; run 2, $m_a = 10$, $m_b = 9.7$, v = 145; run 7, $m_a = 10$, $m_b = 9.7$, v = 145; run 3, $m_a = 20$, $m_b = 19.4$, v = 145; run 6, $m_a = 5$, $m_b = 4.8$, v = 145; run 9, $m_a = 10$, $m_b = 9.7$, v = 145; run 8, $m_a = 5$, $m_b = 4.8$, v = 145. Present these data in a table; make the table as complete and economical as possible.

6.6 Many Nobel-prize winning scientists have also been practicing artists. Here is a partial list: Adrian, physiologist + painter/sketcher; Sherrington, physiologist + poet; Heisenberg, physicist + musician; Ramsay, chemist + poet; Pauling, physical chemist + drafter; Bragg, physicist + painter/sketcher; Alvarez, physicist + musician; Roentgen, physicist + photographer; Feynman, physicist + painter/sketcher; Hoffmann, chemist + poet; McClintock, geneticist + musician; Ostwald, chemist + photographer; Fleming, bacteriologist + painter/sketcher; DeBroglie, physicist + musician; Koch, bacteriologist + photographer; Florey, chemist + painter/sketcher; Herzberg, chemist + musician; Haber, chemist + poet; K. Lorenz, ethologist + painter/sketcher; Alvarez, physicist + drafter; Michelson, physicist + painter/sketcher; Marconi, inventor + musician; Van't Hoff, chemist + poet; Ostwald, physical chemist + painter/sketcher; Michelson, physicist + musician; Ramon y Cajal, neuroanatomist + painter/sketcher; Ramsay, physical chemist + drafter; Florey, chemist + photographer; Einstein, physicist + musician. Organize these data into a table that includes name, profession, and art. Justify the way in which your table presents the data. (Data from R. S. Root-Bernstein [15].)

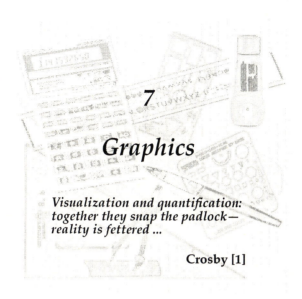

7

Graphics

Visualization and quantification:
together they snap the padlock—
reality is fettered ...

Crosby [1]

Many kinds of technical information are presented most effectively and economically through such graphic devices as plots and charts. Compared to text and equations, graphics are often more effective because they may be more closely akin to the ways people think: the oldest historical records are not text but drawings on bone, rock, and cave walls. Apparently, many people think about technical material, not in words or numbers or equations, but in pictures. The pictures contained in technical graphics are rarely in any sense realistic, and yet their abstract symbolism facilitates communication. For example, to comprehend an equation, readers must make an explicit translation: they must remember what the symbols represent, they must recognize how mathematical operators (+, /, =, etc.) establish relations among the symbols, and they must interpret those symbols and relations in the context of some physical reality. Such a translation is no small task. But less symbolic translation may be required to interpret a well-executed graphic, leaving readers free to concentrate on the meaning of the information itself.

Nowadays computer software substantially reduces the labor of creating plots and charts; or, rather, graphic software reduces the labor of creating first drafts. Unfortunately, easy-to-use software may seduce us into neglecting graphic design, leading us to use a crisply printed first draft as the final copy. But graphics must be created with care, for poorly designed graphics can frustrate a reader's attempts to comprehend, and carelessly executed graphics can lead a reader astray. As always, our goal is to help the reader get the message—just as an effective paragraph is a consequence of much thought and editing, so too is an effective graphic.

7.1 SOME SIMPLE PLOTS AND CHARTS

In this section we describe four kinds of simple graphics: the x-y plot, the dead-man plot, the difference plot, and the dot chart. For more detailed discussions and examples of other kinds of graphic devices, see the books by Tufte [2, 3] and Cleveland [4].

7.1.1 X-Y PLOTS

Of the many graphic devices that are used in scientific and engineering literature, the most common is the x-y plot. These plots are sometimes called line graphs or scatter plots; in any case, such a plot shows how a dependent variable y responds when an independent variable x is changed. An example is shown in Figure 7.1, which presents the population in the U. S. as determined by each federal census from 1780 to 2000.

Usually the scales on each axis are linear, as in Figure 7.1, but if the curve relating x and y is nonlinear, then we may try to straighten the curve by altering the scales. For example, if the relation between x and y is exponential,

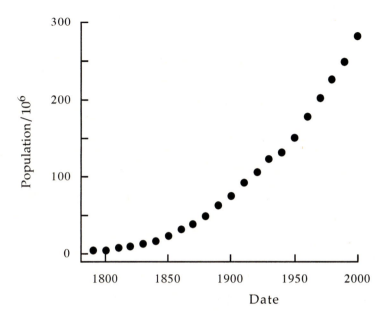

Figure 7.1 Population in the U. S. from 1790 to 2000.

$$y = Ae^{Bx} \qquad (7.1)$$

then a linear relation exists between x and $\ln y$,

$$\ln y = Bx + \ln A \qquad (7.2)$$

and a semilogarithmic plot would yield a straight line. The slope of that line is given by the value of B; so, if two points (x_1, y_1) and (x_2, y_2) are known, then the slope can be computed from

$$B = \frac{\ln y_2 - \ln y_1}{x_2 - x_1} \qquad (7.3)$$

Based on the growth law (5.52) we might expect the population of a young country to grow exponentially, and we test this expectation by replotting the data in Figure 7.1 on the semilogarithmic form of Figure 7.2. From this new figure we see that during the early years of the republic the population did indeed grow exponentially: from 1790 to 1880 the rate of increase was about 3% per year, so the population doubled about every 24 years. But more interestingly, Figure 7.2 suggests that the population grew exponentially throughout the 20th century, though at a lower rate than before. Thus since 1910 the growth rate has been about 1.25% per year, giving a doubling time of about 55 years.

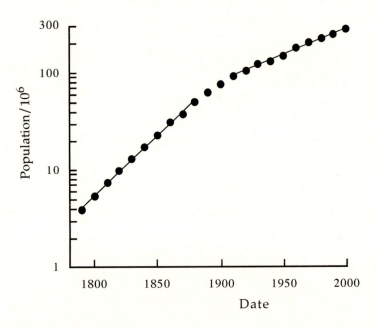

Figure 7.2 Nonlinear scales can sometimes simplify interpretations and presentations of data. Here a semilog plot is used to present the same population data shown in Figure 7.1. The lines are least-squares fits to the form (7.2).

If, instead of an exponential relation, x and y are related by a power law,

$$y = Cx^D \tag{7.4}$$

then a linear relation exists between $\ln x$ and $\ln y$,

$$\ln y = D\ln x + \ln C \tag{7.5}$$

and a log-log plot will yield a straight line. The slope of this line is given by the parameter D, which may be computed from two known points,

$$D = \frac{\ln y_2 - \ln y_1}{\ln x_2 - \ln x_1} \tag{7.6}$$

To illustrate the power law (7.4), we consider how the weight W of fish correlate with length L. For members of the same species we expect individual weights to be proportional to body volume; that is,

$$W = kL^3 \tag{7.7}$$

where the constant k depends on body density and shape. The hypothetical data in Figure 7.3 illustrate (7.7); that is, we expect fish of the same species to be isometric in that their shapes should be the same, independent of size.

Semilog and log-log plots provide convenient ways to obtain straight lines when we know that x and y are related by either an exponential or a power law form. But when we do not know how x and y are related, a trial-and-error procedure must be used to straighten curves. In such cases we can find functions that will

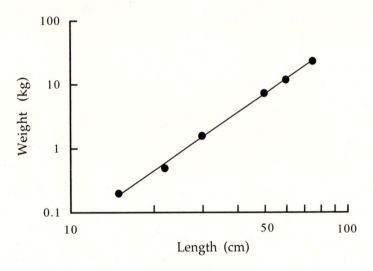

Figure 7.3 If data obey a power law, then the data fall along a straight line when plotted on log-log axes. This plot shows that weight scales with size for the scaleless fish *Symbolous confusious* (nonextant). Points are contrived; line is a least-squares fit to the power-law form (7.7) and has slope = 3.02.

straighten a curve by performing a systematic search through a ladder of algebraic expressions, as discussed by Tukey [5].

7.1.2 DIFFERENCE PLOTS

The x-y plot shows how two different quantities are related. But sometimes we want to compare values of the same quantity obtained from two different sources; this situation often arises when we test a theory by comparing predicted values with measured values. A plot of "predicted values" vs "true values" is sometimes called a *dead-man plot*.

The dead-man plot is also used in calibrating measuring devices. An example is shown in Figure 7.4, which contains the calibration data for a meter that monitors a flow of water through a pipe. In this figure the flow rate on the ordinate was measured using bucket, scales, and stop watch, and therefore some uncertainty pertains to the measured values; however, the error bars are so small that they are obscured by the dots.

If the meter readings and the measured values agreed completely, then the points on a dead-man plot would fall on the diagonal. This is the appeal of a dead-man plot: when two sets of data agree, the points fall on a known straight line. This kind of agreement occurs at the low flow rates in Figure 7.4. However, on dead-man plots small discrepancies are hard to judge: the

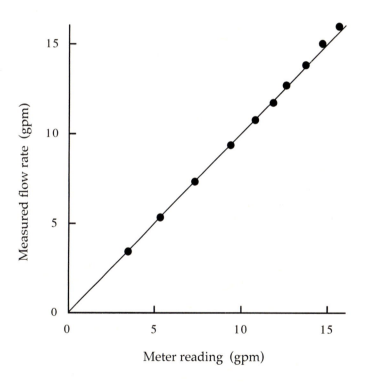

Figure 7.4 Dead-man plot for calibrating a flow meter in a water pipe. The volumetric flow rate is in gallons per minute (gpm); the line is the diagonal $y = x$. Error bars on the measured flow rates are obscured by the dots.

human eye has difficulty estimating the length of a vertical distance between a point and an inclined line. Such small discrepancies occur at high flow rates in Figure 7.4. Further, dead-man plots may be insensitive to small displacements from the diagonal because they often require lengthy scales to capture the full range of data.

To portray small discrepancies we construct a difference plot. For the data in Figure 7.4 we define the difference as

$$\text{difference} = \text{(meter reading)} - \text{(measured flow)} \quad (7.8)$$

With this definition, a positive difference means the meter reads high while a negative difference means it reads low. The differences from Figure 7.4 are plotted in Figure 7.5.

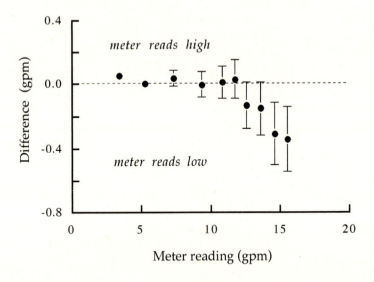

Figure 7.5 A difference plot is often more sensitive to small variations than a simple dead-man plot. This figure contains the difference plot for the calibration curve in Figure 7.4, with the difference defined by (7.8). The error bars represent the 90% confidence level; that is, they are ±2 standard deviations.

Although we could not include error bars on the dead-man plot in Figure 7.4, the ordinate on the difference plot in Figure 7.5 allows us to include uncertainties in the measured flow rates. Using Figure 7.5, we can make a quantitative assessment of the performance of the meter: the meter reads accurately for flow rates up to 12 gallons per minute (gpm), but at higher flows the meter reads low, with the errors reaching about 2.5% at 15 gpm.

7.1.3 DOT CHARTS

Occasionally we need a graphical way to present a set of numbers whose values change with members of a class rather than with some second numerical quantity. In the business community this need is satisfied by pie charts and histograms, but these devices are rarely used in science and engineering. Pie charts and histograms generally represent scalar numbers as areas, which is not only uneconomical but also potentially deceptive. However, we do use histograms to represent probability distributions, wherein both the height and the area carry meaning.

A useful alternative is the *dot chart* [4], which is illustrated in Figure 7.6. Dot charts are usually easier to read when the items on the ordinate are arranged in either ascending or descending order of the quantity plotted on the abscissa. Of course, the scale on the abscissa can be linear or logarithmic, the goal being to spread the dots across the full range of the plotting area.

7.2 MECHANICS OF PRESENTATION

For readers to grasp the information contained in plots and charts, the graphics must be thoughtfully designed and completely documented. Design and documentation are improved by adhering to the guidelines given in this section; this presenta-

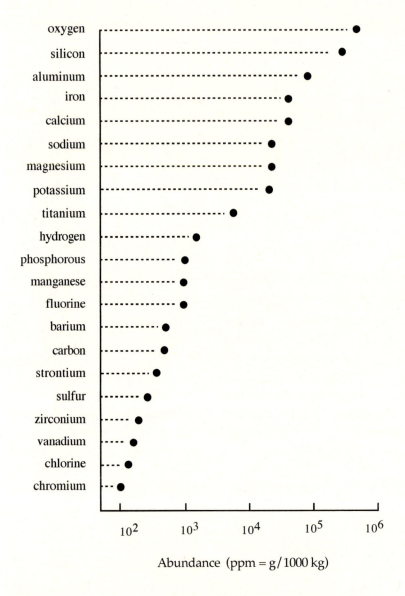

Figure 7.6 A dot chart giving the abundances of the 21 most common elements found in the earth's crust (ppm = parts per million). Note the logarithmic scale on the abscissa. Data taken from [6].

tion has been influenced by the examples and discussions in Tufte [2, 3] and Cleveland [4].

7.2.1 FIGURE NUMBERS AND SUPPORTING TEXT

Each figure should be numbered, cited by number in the text, and presented immediately following its first citation. If a document contains only one figure, then no figure number is required, but the figure should still be cited and discussed in the text. If information is worth a figure, then the figure is worth discussing.

Discussions of figures are motivated by two concerns. First, by presenting information in both graphical and textual formats, we give readers two opportunities to understand. A graphic will appeal to some readers, text will appeal to some others, but in addition, a graphic combined with text will help many. Second, although a picture may be worth a thousand words, such a statement only makes a claim about relative values—it does not necessarily imply an equivalence. Graphics are not like words, and we cannot merely replace a thousand words with one graphic. Graphics and text differ to the extent that they can explicitly draw attention to the writer's message. Every graphic must be supplemented with text that helps readers focus on the figure's important features. Well-designed figures will help convey the message more readily than poorly designed ones, and so poor designs will require more supporting text than good designs.

7.2.2 CAPTION

Captions document the presentation, and that documentation should be complete. In most technical work figures are placed on pages by themselves, separate from the text, and complete documentation allows figures to stand alone. We should not force the reader to search in the text to find the meanings of objects appearing on figures. In some multimedia presentations figures are embedded directly in text, and in those cases, captions may be contained implicitly in the text. But whenever a figure is segregated from text, a complete caption is the best way to help the reader get the message.

The caption of a figure should start with a descriptive title that either states what is plotted, as in Figure 7.1, or states what principal message the figure conveys, as in Figure 7.2. Do not use an uninformative title such as "Plot of y versus x". The descriptive title should be no more than one sentence. Interpretations, discussions, and explanations of unusual behavior should be given in the text, not in a figure caption. The caption should identify any symbols, special lines, ranges of study, units, etc. that are not identified on the axes or on the plotting area. Likewise, the caption should state the meanings of error bars shown with the data, as in Figure 7.5.

7.2.3 ORIENTATION AND SIZE

Figures may be presented either vertically (portrait format) or horizontally (landscape format), but horizontal presentations should be used sparingly because they force the reader to rotate the document to read the figure. If a figure must be presented horizontally, its bottom should appear along the outer edge of the document. That is, on the front of a page, a figure's bottom should be along the right edge; on the back of a page, the bottom should be along the left.

The size of the plotting area should be large enough to contain all the data without crowding, but small enough so that trends are readily apparent. The proportions of the plotting area can often be made appealing: humans seem to prefer objects wider than high, with the ratio of height to width close to the classical golden mean,

$$\frac{\text{height}}{\text{width}} = \frac{\sqrt{5}-1}{2} = 0.618\ldots \tag{7.9}$$

For example, for a 5-inch abscissa the golden mean (7.9) requires a 3.1-inch ordinate. This size is appropriate for a vertical plot on a 8.5 x 11-inch page because the 5-inch width leaves 1.25-inch margins plus one inch for the scale markings and axes label on the ordinate. Of course, other sizes are sometimes preferred; thus, a dead-man plot should usually have the same height and width, as in Figure 7.4, so the $y = x$ reference line is equidistant from ordinate and abscissa.

7.2.4 AXES

Axes should be drawn along the left and bottom of the plotting area. Do not draw axes in such heavy lines that they dominate the plot; the eyes of readers should be drawn to the data, not to the axes. For the same reason, boundary lines along the top and right of the plot should usually be omitted.

Each axis should be labeled with the name of the plotted quantity or the symbol used for the quantity or both. The label should also contain the units and any scale factor that applies to the scale. The notation for scale factors should be the same as that used for scale factors in headings of tables (§ 6.2.4): if the displayed scale has been multiplied by a factor, place that factor in parenthesis in the label; if the scale has been divided by a factor, precede the factor by a solidus in the label. For example, the label on the ordinate in Figure 7.2 indicates that the scale has been divided by one million.

7.2.5 SCALES

Scales should be chosen so that the data span the plotting area. Mark the axes with tics in multiples that are easy for readers to grasp: 2, 4, 5, or 10. Do not use peculiar multiples such as 3, 6, or 15. Tic marks should be long enough to be seen after any reduction of the figure, but they should not be so long that they intrude into the plotting area. Use a small number of tic marks along each axis, and apply numerical labels to only a few tics.

In labeling the scale of an axis, the number of significant figures is not determined by the precision of the data plotted; rather, the number of figures should be no more than the number allowed by the resolution of the scale. For example, consider a linear scale that extends from 0 to 50 with tic marks at 10-unit intervals. If readers can resolve values to one unit, then the tic marks should be labeled 10, 20, 30, 40, 50. Using labels of 10.0, 20.0, etc. would be wrong because those labels imply a resolution of 0.1 unit.

Should linear scales on axes start at zero? The argument for starting at zero is that otherwise readers may be misled as to how quickly the quantity y is changing with x [7]. The argument against is that the data should fill the plotting area, and technically informed readers will not be misled by the lack of zeroes on axes [4]. The latter argument seems more sensible to me, but your first concern is always the reader. If your readers may be led astray without zeroes, then start the scales at zero.

7.2.6 DATA

By convention, measured data are presented as symbols with error bars; theoretical predictions and correlations are usually presented as lines. Symbols should be large enough to be distinguishable after any reduction of the figure. The data should dominate the plotting area; keep axes, legends, and notes away from the data. All lines and symbols must be identified on the figure: in a label on the plotting area, in a legend, or in the caption.

Overlapping data present special problems that require extra attention: do not let one set of data obscure another set.

Overlaps can sometimes be made visible by using broken lines or partial symbols. If two symbols directly overlap, consider using an enlarged open symbol for one datum so it can completely circumscribe a smaller symbol for the other. These suggestions apply to overlaps of a few points; if two sets of data largely overlap, consider splitting an axis to separate the sets. An example is provided in Figure 5.1.

7.2.7 KEY TO SYMBOLS

If the plot contains more that one set of data, then we must indicate the distinctions. This can be done in three ways. If the data are plotted as curves, then the best way is to label each curve directly. These labels should be placed above the curves; but often there is not sufficient space to place direct labels, or the data may involve points as well as curves. In these situations consider using a legend placed in the plotting area. Be sure the legend is well separated from the data; moreover, do not use large legends that dominate the plotting area and crowd out the data. If a legend interferes with the data, then the third option is to identify curves and symbols in the caption. The caption to Figure 7.2 is an example.

7.2.8 GRIDS

Do not use grids; they conflict with the data and contaminate the plot with useless ink.

7.2.9 FITS TO THE DATA

If the plot contains only measured points, resist the temptation to connect the dots or to draw in a line "merely to guide the eye." Such lines impose a personal interpretation on the data; better to let readers make their own interpretations (see Figure

7.1). But if some basis exists for correlating the data, then a line based on that correlation is justified (see Figure 7.2). After all, a principal purpose of any plot is to make comparisons.

Many graphic software packages make it easy for users to fit polynomials to plotted points. These fitting routines are much abused. Do not fit curves to data without reason: just to show a curve through the points is not reason enough. Legitimate reasons include the testing of a theory or hypothesis, or the development of a correlation that would allow readers to interpolate among the data. In the latter case, you should present the correlating equation in the text as well as show the correlating line on the plot.

In the absence of theoretical guidance, correlating equations should be chosen based on Ockham's razor: *entities should not be multiplied beyond necessity.* Thus, you should choose the correlation that is consistent with the data, within their uncertainties, and that contains the smallest number of adjustable parameters. Recall that a polynomial of degree n contains (n + 1) coefficients and therefore can be made to pass *exactly* through (n + 1) points. For example, if we have two points, then we can always find a first degree polynomial ($n = 1$)

$$y = mx + b \qquad (7.10)$$

that passes exactly through the two points. The two known points allow us to determine values for the slope m and the intercept b.

Similarly, if we have five points, as in Figure 7.7, then we can find a fourth degree polynomial that passes exactly through the points,

$$y = a_o + a_1 x + a_2 x^2 + a_3 x^3 + a_4 x^4 \qquad (7.11)$$

Here the values for the coefficients a_i are to be determined by the curve fit. But often a high-degree polynomial can pass through the points only by introducing oscillations in the curve. Without theoretical or experimental justifications for the oscillations, a high-degree polynomial may be an overly complicated, and perhaps unrealistic, representation of the data: using such polynomials violates Ockham's razor. Thus, for the points in Figure 7.7, a straight line is sufficient to correlate the data, within their uncertainties.

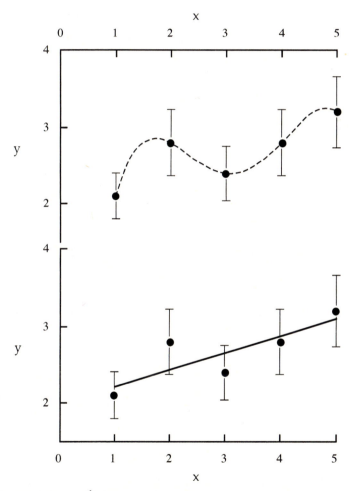

Figure 7.7 An nth-degree polynomial can always be made to pass through $(n+1)$ points (top). But for these points, a straight line is sufficient to correlate the data within their uncertainties (bottom).

7.3 Effective Design

The material in § 7.2 can guide the way we edit plots and charts. Consider Figure 7.7. In the first draft of Figure 7.7 the message was muddled because we used one set of axes to contain the points, the error bars, and both lines. To clarify the presentation we separated the two lines by using two sets of axes, and to keep the plotting area free of distractions, we moved the upper abscissa to the top of the plot. Using multiple axes, as in Figure 7.7, is a standard way to separate data that overlap.

In this section we give examples of poorly designed plots and suggest ways for improving them. The discussion is organized around three themes: When to use plots, How to emphasize the data on plots, and Why plotting the right function can be important.

7.3.1 Is This Plot Really Necessary?

Plots and charts are used to show comparisons: How do theoretical predictions compare with experiment? How does the relation between x and y respond to a change in a parameter? How does a quantity x vary for different members of a class of things? Even when we plot a single curve, we do so to compare one part of the curve to another part. So if you have no comparison to make, then you don't need a plot.

This seems obvious enough, yet it is not uncommon to see plots like the one in Figure 7.8. In this figure nothing changes—the three temperatures are the same within their uncertainties—and so Figure 7.8 is unnecessary: the values would be better reported in the text, or perhaps in a table. Further, the figure has used a disproportionate amount of ink and paper to present six numbers: the three temperatures and their uncertainties. The figure is neither necessary nor economical.

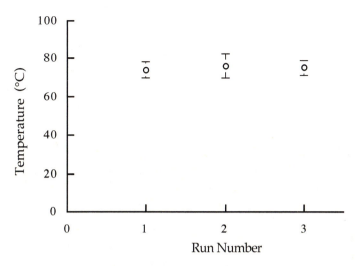

Figure 7.8 When the data are few and unchanging, as here, then they would be better presented as a table. These points represent temperatures in a chemical reactor at the ends of three different runs of the same reaction.

When should we present data in plots as opposed to text or tables? When we have only two or three values to compare, then the comparison can be done in the text. If we want to emphasize the values, we can set them apart from the text by an implicit table. For example, the values in Figure 7.8 could be presented like this:

Run 1	$74 \pm 4°C$
Run 2	$76 \pm 6°C$
Run 3	$75 \pm 4°C$

More generally, we should use tables when exact numerical values are needed, either for *quantitative* comparisons or for quantitative documentation of the results of an experiment or a calculation. Plots and charts are used to make *qualitative* comparisons. Don't expect readers to extract accurate numbers from plots and don't expect them to discover patterns from simple tables of numbers. If you want to use a table to reveal a pattern, then the table must be designed in a special way; one example occurs in the special organization of Rayleigh's data shown in Table 6.11b.

7.3.2 EMPHASIZE THE DATA

In any plot or chart the main focus of attention should be the data. Don't allow the structure of a plot—its axes, labels, and other paraphernalia—to dominate the plot and thereby draw the reader's attention away from the data. In this section we show several common ways that careless writers have found to undermine the messages their plots are intended to convey.

One way is to choose scales inappropriately, confining the data to a small region, as in Figure 7.9a. In this figure the scales

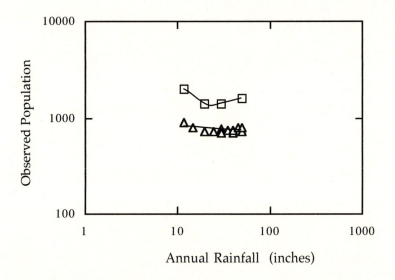

Figure 7.9a Choose scales that spread the points across the entire plotting area. This plot attempts to show how rain affects the populations of deciduous hippogriffs (squares) and variegated hippogriffs (triangles).

leave too much unused white space around the data, the vertical scale forces some symbols to overlap, the lines through the points are unidentified, and the axes at the top and right are unnecessary. These problems have been corrected in Figure 7.9b. Thus in the edited version the new scales spread the points over the range of the plot, the points have been filled to make them conspicuous, the unnecessary lines have been removed, and the shapes of the plotting symbols have been changed to prevent overlaps.

In Figure 7.9a the data are hidden in the midst of a deserted plain, but more often writers hide their data in a forest of useless embellishments. Such unnecessary additions Tufte has called *chartjunk* [2], because they add clutter without adding insight. A typical example appears in Figure 7.10a. This figure is dominated by unnecessary boxes: a box around the entire plot, a box around the plotting area, and a box around the legend. The figure is also overburdened with too many numerical labels along the axes and with both a title and a caption. If we look

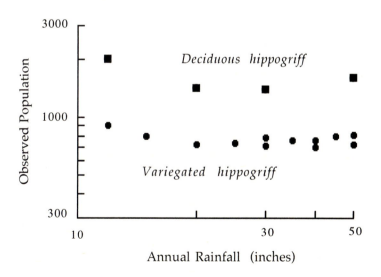

Figure 7.9b Changing the scales and resizing the axes improve Figure 7.9a.

beyond the chartjunk to the data, we see that the points fall close to the vertical and horizontal axes, and in some cases the axes actually overlap points; such behavior suggests the need for a scale change. Finally note that the lines through the points in Figure 7.10a are unidentified; apparently they merely connect the symbols.

These deficiencies are corrected in Figure 7.10b: the chartjunk has been removed, the plot has been changed to a semilog form, and the symbols have been filled to make the points stand out. Further, the legend in Figure 7.10a has been replaced by labels applied directly to the plotting symbols; this is the best way to label data, but it can be done only when sufficient space is available in the plotting area.

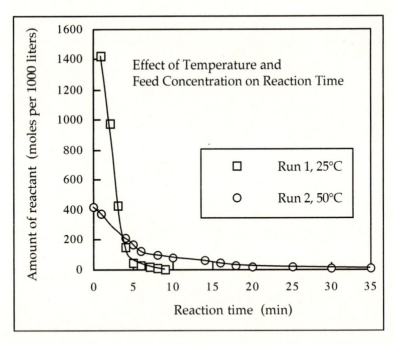

Figure 7.10a Uninformative embellishments and even the axes can obscure data. This plot is intended to show how feed temperature and composition affect the time required for a certain chemical reaction.

In Figure 7.10b both the vertical and horizontal scales have been extended slightly beyond the range of the data, so no points coincide with an axis. In this semilog form each set of data appears to fall roughly on a straight line, and this observation is tested by fitting the data to the exponential form (7.1). The fitted lines are included on the plot. It is a matter of judgement whether those lines correlate the data; that judgement should include an assessment of the uncertainties in the data, but the original authors offer no uncertainties for the data in Figure 7.10a.

The possible forms and kinds of chartjunk seem to be limited only by the devious creativity of the human mind, but if that creativity is momentarily lacking, then we can succumb to the convenience of the computer. Consider the plot in Figure 7.11a, which is a pure product of the computer age: the data were col-

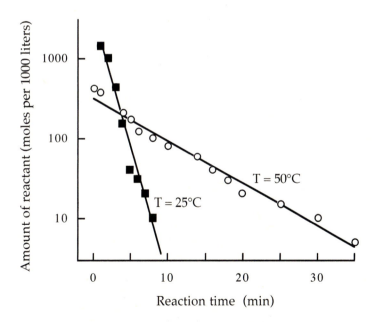

Figure 7.10b Removing the embellishments and changing the ordinate to a log scale improve Figure 7.10a. The lines here are least-squares fits to the exponential form (7.1).

lected by a computer that directly monitored the experiment, and then those numbers were transferred electronically to plotting software, which produced the graph—data untouched by human hands. This plot provides another example of a graphic burdened with superfluous structure: the grid, the axes at the top and right of the plot, and the confusing legend. But more insidious are the plotting symbols, which are all so similar that they are a challenge to differentiate. The confusion is compounded by the overlapping symbols near the origin: although a computer collects many numbers at finely spaced intervals, we do not necessarily help readers by showing all those numbers.

The data in Figure 7.11a suggest that, like Figure 7.10a, a scale change is appropriate. The concentrations start at the origin, increase quickly at short times, and reach a plateau at long times; this is behavior characteristic of a power law (7.4). Thus

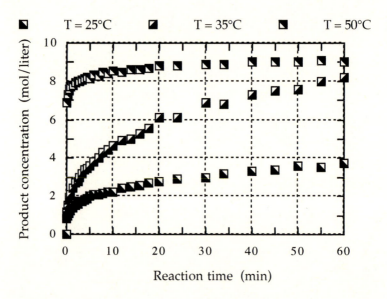

Figure 7.11a In this figure the grid, similar symbols, and overlapping objects frustrate the reader's attempts to see the data. This plot is intended to show how temperature affects the amount of product produced by a certain chemical reaction.

in editing Figure 7.11a we changed to a log-log plot, which does in fact separate the points, apparently along straight lines; see Figure 7.11b. In this edited version we have removed the chart-junk, replaced the legend with labels directly on the data, and moved the axes away from the points. We also added fitted lines to test our presumption that the points obey a power law. The lesson from Figure 7.11a seems clear: computers are indeed labor-saving devices, but using a computer does not excuse us from thinking about what we are doing or reflecting on what it means.

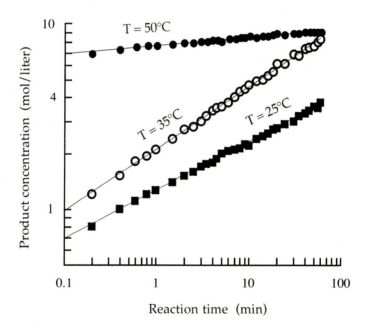

Figure 7.11b Removing the grid and changing to a log-log plot clarify Figure 7.11a. The lines here are least-squares fits of the data to the power-law form (7.4).

7.3.3 PLOT THE RIGHT FUNCTION OF THE DATA

The presentations in Figures 7.10a and 7.11a were improved by changing the functions plotted, but it is not only the presentation that can be helped by a change of function. In § 6.3.4 we showed that a properly designed table can reveal patterns that might otherwise remain undiscovered; this comment also applies to plots and charts. That is, we should design figures not only to be easily read, but also to reveal hidden features and patterns. Often patterns do not become obvious in first drafts of plots; several drafts may be required before a hidden trend becomes apparent.

To illustrate, we consider vapor pressures of water; the following analysis is taken largely from Tukey [5]. For water, vapor pressures change with temperature as shown in Figure 7.12; for example, at 100°C the vapor pressure is exactly 1 atm. The points in Figure 7.12 appear to fall on a smooth curve, but to explore the data we seek a scale change that would straighten the curve.

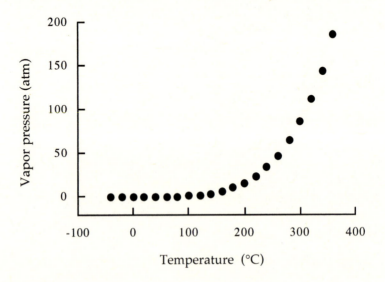

Figure 7.12 Vapor pressures of water, taken from steam tables.

Elementary thermodynamics suggests that pure vapor pressures P are related to the absolute temperature T by

$$\ln P = A - \frac{B}{T} \qquad (7.12)$$

So we replot the points in Figure 7.12 in the form ln P vs 1/T, obtaining Figure 7.13. The points do fall close to a straight line, and if we perform a least-squares fit, we obtain values for the slope (–B) and the intercept A. The resulting line (7.12) is also shown in Figure 7.13. Figure 7.13 and Equation (7.12) are standard ways to represent the vapor pressures of pure substances, and as far as issues of presentation go, Figure 7.13 proves satisfactory. Note for example, how an upper horizontal scale is used to show the original temperatures that are equivalent to the unfamiliar reciprocal temperatures actually plotted.

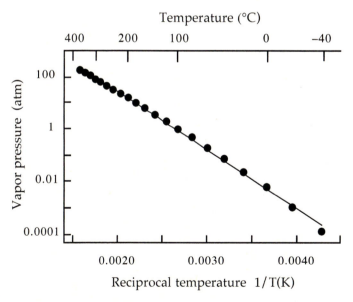

Figure 7.13 Vapor pressures of water nearly fall on a straight line when plotted in the form (7.12). Points are from Figure 7.12; line is a least-squares fit to Equation (7.12)

But if we look more closely at Figure 7.14, we see that although the form (7.12) provides a good representation of the points, it is not perfect. The points deviate some from the line, and those deviations appear to be systematic. To study those discrepancies, we form the differences

$$\text{difference} = \ln P - \ln P_{fit} \qquad (7.13)$$

where P is the true vapor pressure at a temperature T and P_{fit} is the value calculated from (7.12) at the same T. In other words, the values of P are given by the points in Figure 7.13 and the values of P_{fit} are given by the line. These differences are plotted in Figure 7.14.

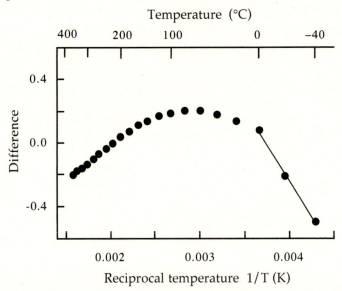

Figure 7.14 For the vapor pressures of water, a difference plot is sufficiently sensitive to reveal an important feature that remains hidden in Figures 7.12 and 7.13: at 0°C liquid water freezes to ice. The differences here were calculated from (7.13); that is, they are the differences between the logarithms of the actual vapor pressures and the fitted ones. The line is a least-squares fit to the three differences at 0°, –20°, and –40°C.

From 360° down to 0°C the differences vary in a smooth systematic fashion. But at 0°C the differences change abruptly from a smooth curve to a straight line. Something happens to the vapor pressures at 0°C—oh yes, at 0°C water freezes. So the vapor pressures from 360° to 0°C are for liquid water, while those from 0° to -40°C are for ice.

Thus the original data in Figure 7.12 conceal a physically important phenomenon: the phase change between liquid and solid. To reveal the phase change we need to plot a function that is more sensitive than those plotted in either Figure 7.12 or 7.13; that is, in this example the difference plot amplifies a signal that is latent in the data. Of course not every plot conceals an important pattern, but some do, and those patterns will remain concealed unless we make explicit efforts to find them.

7.4 SUMMARY

With the computer software now available, we can readily create plots and charts that both supplement and enhance technical presentations. But no matter whether we create graphics by hand or by computer, the fundamental principles of effective and economical design apply. In particular, style must not be dictated by the idiosyncrasies of software; instead, from the options provided by software we must choose those that achieve clear presentations. As you edit plots and charts to improve clarity, keep in mind the following precautions:

(a) Avoid showing the wrong information. Check that symbols, lines, scales, and axes are properly labeled. Check that values of parameters are stated correctly.

(b) Avoid incomplete and confusing information. Cite sources for all data, and state the meanings of all lines. Symbols representing measured values should contain error bars, or a statement about the uncertainties should be included in the caption.

(c) Avoid misleading information. Check that scales do not convey a false sense of how a curve changes over the range of the plot. Avoid imposing subjective interpretations such as lines that "guide the eye."

(d) Avoid concealing information. The amount of information shown on a figure should be commensurate with the amount of ink used: eliminate chartjunk.

EXERCISES

7.1 For temperatures between 200 K and 400 K, plot °C vs K and °F vs K on the same axes. (a) Should your two lines be straight? Why? (b) Mark the normal boiling and melting points of water on each line. (c) What is the value and significance of the slope of each line? (d) Do the two lines intersect? If so, what is the significance of their intersection?

7.2 Use the data in Problem 6.2 to create a dot chart for Reynolds numbers of moving animals. Justify your choice of scale for the abscissa.

7.3 Use the data in Table 6.2 to plot each planet's period of revolution about the sun (in earth years) against the planet's mean distance from the sun (in astronomical units (au), 1 au = mean distance from earth to sun). Your plot should be in a form to give a straight line. What is the value of the slope of your line? This relation was first discovered by Kepler and served as the basis for Newton's universal law of gravitation.

7.4 The heating value of wood depends on moisture content. For wood containing water in various amounts, heating values are as follows:

mass % moisture	10	20	30	40	50	60
Heating value (MJ/kg)	18.6	16.7	14.0	13.2	9.0	6.8

Wood containing more than 67% moisture will not ignite; air-dried wood contains about 15% moisture. Create a plot of these data, using % moisture as the independent variable. Use your plot to estimate the heating value of wood that contains no moisture. (Data from V. Smil[8].)

7.5 The maximum possible speed of a displacement-hull sailboat is limited by the speed of the wave it creates; maximum speed is related to hull length by,

$$s = \frac{4\sqrt{L}}{3} \tag{7.14}$$

where L = length (in feet) of hull at waterline and s = maximum speed in knots. (1 knot = 1 nautical mile/hour = 2000 yards/hour.)

(a) Plot the maximum speed for boats having hull lengths between 10 and 100 feet. The form of your plot should yield a straight line. What is the value of the slope of your line? What are the units of your slope?

(b) If you want to double the speed, by how much must you increase the length? The capital cost of a sailboat is proportional to volume, not length, so if you want to double the speed, by (approximately) how much will the initial cost increase?

7.6 The following table contains normal melting points (Mpt) for nineteen straight-chain hydrocarbons:

Substance	Formula	Mpt (K)
ethane	C_2H_6	89.9
propane	C_3H_8	85.5
butane	C_4H_{10}	134.8
pentane	C_5H_{12}	143.4
hexane	C_6H_{14}	177.8
heptane	C_7H_{16}	182.6
octane	C_8H_{18}	216.4
nonane	C_9H_{20}	219.7
decane	$C_{10}H_{22}$	243.5
undecane	$C_{11}H_{24}$	247.6
dodecane	$C_{12}H_{26}$	263.6
tridecane	$C_{13}H_{28}$	267.8
tetradecane	$C_{14}H_{30}$	279.0
pentadecane	$C_{15}H_{32}$	283.0
hexadecane	$C_{16}H_{34}$	291.0
heptadecane	$C_{17}H_{36}$	295.0
octadecane	$C_{18}H_{38}$	301.3
nonadecane	$C_{19}H_{40}$	305.
eicosane	$C_{20}H_{42}$	310.

Plot these temperatures vs the number of carbon atoms per molecule. Do your data fall on a single curve? If not, can you replot the data so as to emphasize the differences?

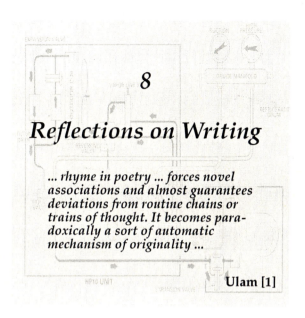

8

Reflections on Writing

> *... rhyme in poetry ... forces novel associations and almost guarantees deviations from routine chains or trains of thought. It becomes paradoxically a sort of automatic mechanism of originality ...*
>
> **Ulam [1]**

Here are three short essays that confront certain problems encountered in the act of writing and that seem to bear on the development of style.

8.1 UPPING THE ANTE

In his book, *On Writing Well,* William Zinsser observes that writers seem to fall into one of two groups: those who can, with modest effort, generate text relatively quickly and the rest of us, who must labor over every sentence [2]. Writers in the first group tend to find writing a "release", while those in the second find it an agony. Although the aptitudes of these two groups seem very different, members of both groups produce good (and bad) writing. That is, ease or difficulty of writing does not seem to affect the quality of what is written. The question is, what causes these two different ways of writing?

At first we might suppose that these two groups separate novices from experts: perhaps novices labor for lack of experience, while experts have developed the skills that allow them to breeze competently through their work. But when we look into the two groups, we find that both contain some novices and some experts. In fact, it appears that experts are more likely than novices to struggle with their craft. Apparently it is not the amount of experience that necessarily separates one group from the other; instead, the distinction seems to lie in the goals writers set for themselves [3].

One way to distinguish goals is to separate knowledge *transmission* from knowledge *transformation*. In knowledge transmission the goal is to communicate what a writer knows about a subject. Therefore, the problems faced during writing are more of form than of content; that is, the writer largely concentrates on finding a way to organize the presentation so the material is readily grasped by readers. Knowledge transmission is the mode typically assumed by students writing theses; a student may spend years acquiring knowledge of a subject, and the thesis serves as a vehicle for documenting and transmitting that acquired knowledge.

But in knowledge transformation the act of writing becomes a way to search for new insights, new connections, and new interpretations of material. Thus the goal is to deepen understanding for both writer and reader. In knowledge transformation writers must struggle with both form and content: form to achieve clarity and content to achieve originality. As a writer gains experience, knowledge transmission may become easier, but knowledge transformation is always difficult because the writer is attempting something new.

It seems likely that most individuals may write in either mode—transmission or transformation—depending on the importance of the project and on the writer's familiarity with the material. And so it would seem useful, when planning a project, for writers to articulate whether the work is to be one of transmission or of transformation. In many cases, such as reports, procedures, and theses, knowledge transmission is all that is either necessary or desirable, and it would be foolish to attack these projects in a transformation mode.

But while many writers can probably function in both modes, any individual may have a predilection for one or the other. In transformation mode writers find their craft an agony because they continuously elevate the standards they set for themselves, much as an athlete continuously raises the bar on the high jump. Thus,

> ... expert writers' systematic escalation of problem complexity ensures that writing remains a difficult task ... [3]

So if you find writing difficult, you may benefit from discovering why it seems difficult. Is it for lack of knowledge of the subject? If so, there is no help except to apply yourself to acquire the necessary knowledge. Is it for lack of writing experience? If so, then practise writing. Start with small projects: a summary of a newspaper article or a paragraph describing something you can see right now. Practise editing as well: edit old work of your own, and edit paragraphs written by others.

But if you find writing difficult because of what you aim to accomplish, then consider whether the benefits of success will justify the effort required. Ultimately this is a judgement only you can make. Keep in mind that every creative act proceeds by trial and error, and few trial-and-error searches are guaranteed to succeed. Every attempt at creativity is a gamble—and there is a time to fold, a time to stand pat, and a time to raise the level of commitment.

8.2 Easy Writing Makes Cursed Hard Reading†

A wind of dissatisfaction now blows across academia in reaction to the discovery that many college students cannot write a coherent paragraph. This deficiency is being addressed in educationally progressive ways: workshops and seminars are being held for instructors, English departments are revising syllabi, and in some universities writing activities are being imposed in technical courses. In short, many educators seem preoccupied with plans and schemes, but few seem engaged in helping students improve. Oft unrecognized exceptions are science and engineering instructors, some of whom still mark reports from laboratory experiments and design projects.

But can we do more? Perhaps we can, but not by attaching undue value to those abstractions that are the common currency of committees, workshops, and focus groups. For example, in one such abstraction we are asked to view the act of writing as a kind of problem, akin to the mechanical problem of getting words onto paper, as if writing were synonymous with word processing. Here we may have encountered a red herring, for while certain mechanical and psychological devices appear to ease the act of writing, such devices are often employed at the expense of the reader, whose plight remains as precarious as ever.

In one of his elegant essays on education, Jacques Barzun [4] has noted that we mislead ourselves by regarding most educational issues as problems, because "problem" brings to mind "solution"—the problem of poor writing can be solved, if only we do such-and-such. In fact the act of writing is not so much a

---

† The title is a line from English playwright Richard Sheridan (1751-1816). An earlier version of § 8.2 was first published in *Chemical Engineering Education* [5]; reprinted here with permission from the Chemical Engineering Division of the American Society of Engineering Education.

problem to be solved as it is a difficulty to be overcome. A problem, once solved, ceases to be an issue and we can move on to other things. But a difficulty, like writing (and teaching), has no solution; the difficulty must be faced and overcome, again and again.

But even if we accept that writing is invariably difficult, we can hope to alleviate the difficulties by certain activities. One help is to encourage good editing, for editing means self-criticism, which in turn can lead to self-improvement. Editing often provides much of the pedagogical value in writing, for it is during editing that writers confront their understanding of the subject and decide how the message can be presented so as to be most easily grasped by their readers.

A second help is to encourage good reading: no one has written well who failed to read well. It is here that students of science and engineering may seem most deprived, for what technical literature is well written? Can we identify a body of writing that will inspire young scientists and engineers? Should we allow students to graduate having read nothing technical, nothing except textbooks? If we subscribe to the idea that engineers must synthesize knowledge from diverse areas, shouldn't engineering students read technical material beyond their specialties? If students must assimilate more information than can be fit into a four-year degree program, won't their chances for future success be improved by the habit of reading?

In grappling with such questions, it seemed worthwhile to compile a short list of books, books well-written and with a technical bent. The list, or some part of it, would implicitly illustrate good writing, and further, the list might lead students to see that it is possible to take delight, both serious and whimsical, in technical things.

My list evolves; the current version is given in the Bibliography. The principal criterion for inclusion is only this: the play of ideas, coupled with the author's use of language, must be such that the book sustains interest on second and even third readings. Most of the books are appropriate for readers above the sophomore level. Few readers will develop a liking for every book in the list, but many should find at least a few congenial companions.

One purpose of the list is to illustrate that a body of well-written literature does exist and is accessible to the technically informed reader. A second purpose is to inspire readers to explore the literature. My list is only a small, idiosyncratic set from a growing collection—know your library. Students can start their explorations with the authors cited in the list: many have written other books, some in similar, others in more technical veins. A third purpose is an attempt, however modest, to encourage scholarly activity. We in academia seem to have misplaced the idea that a primary purpose of advanced study is scholarship, and all scholarly activity is rooted in reading.

8.3 The Rules of Style

Although the rules of English grammar are largely sacrosanct, the conventions of style are largely guidelines—codified suggestions that seem to work much of the time but which may be violated with impunity under the provocation of a creative impulse. But the creative impulse encompasses an element of the paradoxical: creativity seems to flourish only in the shadow of acknowledged rules of constraint. A composer does not confront a keyboard with a vague intention of composing some undefined piece of music; rather, a composer struggles under a clearly articulated intention to create a sonata, or a concerto, or a piece of progressive jazz in rondo form. Such structures impose well-defined constraints under which the composer seeks to be original. Only after the composer has mastered several such forms has he gained the knowledge and experience, and therefore earned the right, to throw off the constraints—to break the rules.

Similar comments seem to apply to all creative activities, including writing. Until writers have mastered the rules of grammar and conventions of style, they are best advised to exercise their creativity within the confines of those rules and conventions. With mastery comes the freedom to break the rules and conventions—not to ignore them, but to violate them with a clear understanding and purpose.

Nevertheless, the conventions of style cited in previous chapters are only guidelines, not rules. I doubt that any precise rules of style exist, though some general rules seem to pertain. But now we approach the realm of semantics in which I find it hard to distinguish general rules from mere conventions. However, if you insist on rules rather than conventions, if you absolutely must have rules of style to write with confidence, then let me offer you the following two, paraphrased from George Polya [6]:

Rule 1:   Have something to say.

Rule 2:   Exercise control; for example, when you have two things to say, say one and then the other, not both at the same time.

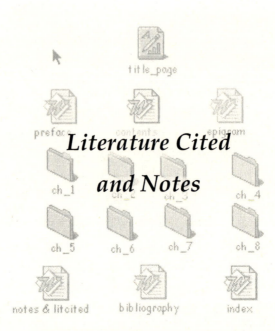

title_page

preface   contents   epigram

Literature Cited

and Notes

ch_1   ch_2   ch_3   ch_4

ch_5   ch_6   ch_7   ch_8

notes & litcited   bibliography   index

CHAPTER 1: WORDS AND PHRASES

[1] Marvin Minsky, *The Society of Mind*, Simon & Schuster, New York, 1986, p. 247.

[2] J. M. Williams, *Style*, 2nd ed., Scott, Foresman and Company, Glenview, IL, 1985.

[3] *Webster's Ninth New Collegiate Dictionary*, Merriam-Webster Inc., Springfield, MA, 1986.

[4] D. R. Hofstadter, *Gödel, Escher, Bach: An Eternal Golden Braid*, Vintage, New York, 1980.

[5] "Delete Unnecessary Words" is a paraphrase of Rule 17 in Strunk and White: "Omit Needless Words." The intention is to emphasize that we reduce the number of words mainly by deleting during editing, not by omitting during drafting. W. Strunk, Jr. and E. B. White, *The Elements of Style*, 3rd ed., Macmillan, New York, 1979.

CHAPTER 2: STRONG SENTENCES

[1] Arthur Quinn, *Figures of Speech*, Gibbs M. Smith, Inc., Salt Lake City, 1982.

[2] W. H. Press, B. P. Flannery, S. A. Teukolsky, and W. T. Vetterling, *Numerical Recipes*, Cambridge University Press, Cambridge, 1986.

[3] *Webster's Ninth New Collegiate Dictionary*, Merriam-Webster Inc., Springfield, MA, 1986.

[4] *The American Heritage Dictionary of the English Language*, 3rd ed., Houghton Mifflin Co., Boston, 1992.

[5] *Oxford English Dictionary*, 2nd ed., Clarendon Press, Oxford, 1989.

[6] H. W. Fowler, *A Dictionary of Modern English Usage*, 2nd ed., revised by Sir Ernest Gowers, Oxford University Press, Oxford, 1983, p. 689.

[7] The name *linkage* is taken from Jacques Barzun, *Simple & Direct*, Harper & Row, New York, 1975.

[8] H. Petroski, *To Engineer is Human*, Vintage, New York, 1992.

CHAPTER 3: COHERENT PARAGRAPHS

[1] L. Cooper, *An Introduction to the Meaning and Structure of Physics*, Harper & Row, New York, 1968.

[2] P. W. Atkins, *Molecules*, W. H. Freeman, New York, 1987, p. 24; volume 21 in the Scientific American Library Series.

[3] J. B. Fenn, *Engines, Energy, and Entropy*, W. H. Freeman and Co., San Francisco, 1982, p. 125.

[4] E. O. Wilson, *The Diversity of Life*, W. W. Norton and Co., New York, 1992, p. 145.

[5] H. Petroski, *To Engineer is Human*, Vintage, New York, 1992, p. 201.

[6] H. Wiencek, *The World of LEGO® Toys*, Harry N. Abrams, Inc., New York, 1987, p. 71-2.

[7] V. F. Weisskopf, *Knowledge and Wonder*, MIT Press, Cambridge, MA, 1980, p. 175.

CHAPTER 4: PUNCTUATION

[1] Marvin Minsky, *The Society of Mind*, Simon & Schuster, New York, 1986, p. 127.

[2] J. C. Hodges (ed.), *Harbrace College Handbook*, 12th ed., Harcourt Brace Jovanovich, Fort Worth, 1994.

[3] J. S. Dodd (ed.), *The ACS Style Guide*, American Chemical Society, Washington, D. C., 1986.

[4] V. F. Weisskopf, *Knowledge and Wonder*, 2nd ed., MIT Press, Cambridge, MA, 1980, p. 175.

CHAPTER 5: EQUATIONS

[1] R. Feynman, *The Character of Physical Law*, MIT Press, Cambridge, MA, 1967, p. 40.

[2] Section 5.1 has been influenced by Polya's comments on the importance of a good notation: G. Polya, *How To Solve It*, 2nd ed., Princeton University Press, Princeton, NJ, 1957, p. 134f.

[3] Section 5.2 is drawn from *The Chicago Manual of Style*, 13th ed., University of Chicago Press, Chicago, 1982, and *A Guide for Wiley-Interscience and Ronald Press Authors*, 2nd ed., John Wiley & Sons, New York, 1979.

[4] J. D. van der Waals, *On the Continuity of the Gaseous and Liquid States*, J. S. Rowlinson, ed., North-Holland, Amsterdam, 1988.

[5] There is evidence that the Pythagorean theorem was known in ancient Egypt, Babylonia, India, and China, long before Pythagoras (580-500 BC). See B. L. van der Waerden, *Geometry and Algebra in Ancient Civilizations*, Springer-Verlag, Berlin, 1983, or O. Neugebauer, *The Exact Sciences in Antiquity*, 2nd ed., Harper & Brothers, New York, 1962.

[6] J. Rosen, *A Symmetry Primer for Scientists*, John Wiley & Sons, New York, 1983.

[7] R. P. Feynman, R. B. Leighton, and M. Sands, *The Feynman Lectures on Physics*, vol. 1, Addison-Wesley, Reading, MA, 1963, p. 35-5f.

[8] At least one Arabic commentator claims that Archimedes (287-212 BC) was the first to obtain Heron's formula for the area of a triangle; see B. L. van der Waerden, *Geometry and Algebra in Ancient Civilizations*, Springer-Verlag, Berlin, 1983, p. 183f.

CHAPTER 6: TABLES

[1] Artur Schnabel, quoted in M. Minsky, *The Society of Mind*, Simon & Schuster, New York, 1986, p. 52.

[2] J. W. Tukey, *Exploratory Data Analysis*, Addison-Wesley, Reading, MA, 1977.

[3] P. W. Atkins, *Molecules*, Scientific American Library Series, No. 21, W. H. Freeman, New York, 1987.

[4] Properties of Group VI hydrides were taken from Yu. Ya. Fialkov, *The Extraordinary Properties of Ordinary Solutions*, Mir Publishers, Moscow, 1985.

[5] Planetary data from W. K. Hamblin and E. H. Christiansen, *Exploring the Planets*, Macmillan, New York, 1990, except values for the minimum and maximum distances from the sun,

which are from C. W. Tombaugh and P. Moore, *Out of the Darkness,* Lutterworth Press, Guildford, Surrey, 1980, p. 29.

[6] P. B. Medawar and J. S. Medawar, *Aristotle to Zoos,* Harvard University Press, Cambridge, MA, 1983, p. 68.

[7] T. T. Perls, "The Oldest Old," *Scientific American,* 272 (1), 70 (1995).

[8] The correlation for mixture critical temperatures was originally given by R. B. Grieves and G. Thodos, *AIChE Journal,* 8, 550 (1962). The numerical values for the coefficients A_{ij} are from R. C. Reid and T. K. Sherwood, *The Properties of Gases and Liquids,* 2nd ed., McGraw-Hill, New York, 1966, p. 355.

[9] *Rand McNally Road Atlas,* Rand McNally & Co., Chicago, 1987, p. 105.

[10] Section 6.2 is drawn from *The Chicago Manual of Style,* 13th ed., University of Chicago Press, Chicago, 1982.

[11] These figures of speech were extracted from Arthur Quinn, *Figures of Speech,* Gibbs M. Smith, Inc., Salt Lake City, 1982.

[12] Lord Rayleigh, *Proceedings of the Royal Society,* 55, 340 (1894); reprinted in *Scientific Papers by Lord Rayleigh,* Dover, New York, vol. IV, 104 (1964).

[13] V. Smil, *Energies,* MIT Press, Cambridge, MA, 1999, p. xvi.

[14] S. Vogel, *Life in Moving Fluids,* Princeton University Press, Princeton, NJ, 1983, p. 67.

[15] R. S. Root-Bernstein, *Discovering,* Harvard University Press, Cambridge, MA, 1989, p. 318f.

CHAPTER 7: GRAPHICS

[1] A. W. Crosby, *The Measure of Reality,* Cambridge University Press, Cambridge, 1997, p. 229.

[2] E. R. Tufte, *The Visual Display of Quantitative Information*, Graphics Press, Cheshire, CN, 1983.

[3] E. R. Tufte, *Envisioning Information*, Graphics Press, Cheshire, CN, 1990.

[4] W. S. Cleveland, *The Elements of Graphing Data*, Wadsworth, Monterey, CA, 1985.

[5] J. W. Tukey, *Exploratory Data Analysis*, Addison-Wesley, Reading, MA, 1977.

[6] J. Emsley, *The Elements*, 2nd ed., Clarendon Press, Oxford, 1991.

[7] H. Petroski, "Soft Graphics," *American Scientist*, 83 (1), 17 (1995).

[8] V. Smil, *Energies*, MIT Press, Cambridge, MA, 1999, p. 117.

CHAPTER 8: REFLECTIONS ON WRITING

[1] S. M. Ulam, *Adventures of a Mathematician*, Scribner, New York, 1983.

[2] W. Zinsser, *On Writing Well*, 3rd ed., Harper & Row, New York, 1985.

[3] M. Bryson, C. Bereiter, M. Scardamalia, and E. Joram, "Going Beyond the Problem as Given: Problem Solving in Expert and Novice Writers," in *Complex Problem Solving: Principles and Mechanisms*, R. J. Sternberg and P. A. Frensch, eds., Lawrence Erlbaum Associates, Hillsdale, NJ, 1991.

[4] Jacques Barzun, *Begin Here*, University of Chicago Press, Chicago, 1991.

[5] J. M. Haile, "Easy Writing Makes Hard Reading," *Chemical Engineering Education*, 28 , 278 (1994).

[6] G. Polya, *How To Solve It*, 2nd ed., Princeton University Press, Princeton, NJ, 1957, p. 172-3.

Bibliography of Selected Technical Literature

BOOKS AND ARTICLES FOR INSTRUCTION

I. Asimov, "Hints" and "The Mosaic and the Plate Glass," in *Asimov on Science Fiction*, Doubleday, New York, 1981.

G. D. Gopen and J. Swan, "The Science of Scientific Writing," *American Scientist*, 78 , 550 (1990).

W. Strunk, Jr. and E. B. White, *The Elements of Style*, 3rd ed., Macmillan, New York, 1979.

L. Thomas, "Notes on Punctuation," in *The Medusa and the Snail*, Viking Press, New York, 1979.

Edward R. Tufte, *The Visual Display of Quantitative Information*, Graphics Press, Cheshire, Connecticut, 1983.

Edward R. Tufte, *Envisioning Information*, Graphics Press, Cheshire, Connecticut, 1990.

Mark Twain, "Reply to the Editor of 'The Art of Authorship'," in *Mark Twain Collected Tales, Speeches, & Essays*, 1852-1890, Library of America, New York, 1992, p. 945.

Mark Twain, "Fenimore Cooper's Literary Offences," in *Mark Twain Collected Tales, Speeches, & Essays*, 1891-1910, Library of America, New York, 1992, p. 180.

J. M. Williams, *Style*, 2nd ed., Scott, Foresman and Company, Glenview, IL, 1985.

BOOKS FOR INSPIRATION

P. W. Atkins, *Molecules*, W. H. Freeman, New York, 1987; volume 21 in the Scientific American Library Series.

Hans Christian von Baeyer, *Taming the Atom*, Random House, New York, 1992.

Daniel J. Boorstin, *The Discoverers*, Random House, New York, 1983.

William H. Brock, *The Norton History of Chemistry*, W. W. Norton, New York, 1992.

Bryan Bunch, *Reality's Mirror: Exploring the Mathematics of Symmetry*, Wiley, New York, 1989.

A. G. Cairns-Smith, *Seven Clues to the Origin of Life*, Cambridge University Press, Cambridge, 1985.

Leon N. Cooper, *An Introduction to the Meaning and Structure of Physics*, Harper & Row, New York, 1968.

Philip J. Davis, *The Thread*, 2nd Ed., Harcourt Brace Jovanovich, Boston, 1989.

Philip J. Davis and Reuben Hersh, *Descartes' Dream*, Harcourt Brace Jovanovich, New York, 1986.

Freeman Dyson, *Infinite in All Directions*, Harper & Row, New York, 1988.

Loren Eiseley, *The Immense Journey*, Random House, New York, 1957.

Loren Eiseley, *The Unexpected Universe*, Harcourt, Brace, & World, New York, 1969.

John B. Fenn, *Engines, Energy, and Entropy*, W. H. Freeman, San Francisco, 1982.

Richard P. Feynman, Robert B Leighton, and Matthew Sands, *The Feynman Lectures on Physics* (three volumes), Addison-Wesley, Reading, MA, 1963.

Richard P. Feynman, *The Character of Physical Law*, MIT Press, Cambridge, MA, 1967.

Richard P. Feynman, *Surely You're Joking, Mr. Feynman*, Bantam, New York, 1986.

Steven Jay Gould, *The Mismeasure of Man*, W. W. Norton, New York, 1981.

Steven Jay Gould, *Wonderful Life*, W. W. Norton, New York, 1989.

Douglas R. Hofstadter, *Gödel, Escher, Bach*, Vintage Books, New York, 1980.

George Johnson, *In the Palaces of Memory*, Knopf, New York, 1991.

Peter Medawar, *Pluto's Republic*, Oxford University Press, Oxford, 1982.

Marvin Minsky, *The Society of Mind*, Simon and Schuster, New York, 1986.

Henry Petroski, *To Engineer Is Human*, Vintage Books, New York, 1992.

Henry Petroski, *The Evolution of Useful Things*, Vintage Books, New York, 1994.

George Polya, *How To Solve It*, 2nd ed., Princeton University Press, Princeton, NJ, 1973.

Andrew Scott, *Vital Principles: The Molecular Mechanisms of Life*, Basil Blackwell, Oxford, 1988.

Raymond Siever, *Sand*, W. H. Freeman, New York, 1988; volume 24 in the Scientific American Library Series.

Robert Scott Root-Bernstein, *Discovering*, Harvard University Press, Cambridge, MA, 1989.

Lewis Thomas, *The Medusa and the Snail*, Viking Press, New York, 1979.

Lewis Thomas, *The Lives of a Cell*, Viking Press, New York, 1974.

D'Arcy W. Thompson, *On Growth and Form*, Abridged edition edited by J. T. Bonner, Cambridge University Press, Cambridge, 1992.

Steven Vogel, *Life in Moving Fluids*, Princeton University Press, Princeton, New Jersey, 1983.

Steven Vogel, *Life's Devices*, Princeton University Press, Princeton, New Jersey, 1988.

Victor F. Weisskopf, *Knowledge and Wonder*, 2nd ed., MIT Press, Cambridge, MA, 1980.

Edward O. Wilson, *The Diversity of Life*, W. W. Norton, New York, 1992.

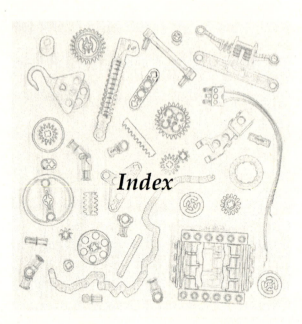

Index

ORDER FORM FOR COPIES OF *TECHNICAL STYLE*

Web Orders: Book orders and credit card payments accepted from our website: http://www.macatea.com/

Postal Orders: Macatea Productions, 217 Todds Creek Road, Central, SC 29630. Enclose a completed copy of this form.

Number of Copies ____ at $29.95 per copy = total of _____

For shipments to addresses in South
Carolina, add 6% sales tax   _____

Shipping & handling
    US: $4 for first copy; $1 for each additional copy
    Int'l: $8 for first copy; $2 for each additional copy   _____

Total Payment Enclosed (check or money order)   _____

Ship to:

Name _____

Street Address/Box #_____

City _____ State ____ Zip _____

Email address _____